She decided that her leaving home would not be just running from somewhere but would be running to some-where. To a large place, a comfortable place, an indoor place, and preferably a beautiful place. And that's why she decided upon the Metropolitan Museum of Art in New York City.

—E. L. Konigsburg,
*From the Mixed-Up Files of
Mrs. Basil E. Frankweiler*

She had a perpetual sense, as she watched the taxi cabs, of being out, out, far out to sea and alone; she always had the feeling that it was very, very dangerous to live even one day.

—Virginia Woolf, *Mrs. Dalloway*

You would not find the boundaries of the soul, though you traveled every road.

—Heraclitus

For nothing is forever and forever and forever, it is not fixed; the earth is always shifting, the light is always changing, the sea does not cease to grind down rock.

—James Baldwin,
Nothing Personal

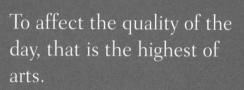

To affect the quality of the day, that is the highest of arts.

—Henry David Thoreau, *Walden*

We finger the world around us with our senses. . . . Our bodies serve to introduce the world to us.

—Anne Truitt, *Turn*

The pleasure of doing a thing in the same way at the same time every day, and sa-vouring it, should be noted.

—Arnold Bennett,
The Journals of Arnold Bennett

Life in Five Senses

CROWN

NEW YORK

Life in Five Senses

How Exploring the Senses
Got Me Out of My Head
and Into the World

Gretchen Rubin

"The more we know,
the more we notice."

Published in the United States by Crown, an
imprint of Random House, a division of
Penguin Random House LLC, New York.

CROWN and the Crown colophon are
registered trademarks of
Penguin Random House LLC.

Hardback ISBN
978-0-593-44274-6
International edition ISBN
978-0-593-72720-1
Ebook ISBN
978-0-593-44275-3

Printed in the
United States
of America
on acid-free
paper

crownpublishing.com

2 4 6 8 9 7 5 3 1

First Edition

Book design by Susan Turner

To Anne Mercogliano

Nobody really looks at anything; it's too hard.

—ANDY WARHOL

Contents

Life in Five Senses

Seeing What Was Missing

◎ 〰 ⃝ ⃝ ⃝

A FEW YEARS AGO, AN ORDINARY EVENT SHOOK UP MY LIFE.
I made a trip to the eye doctor.

One wintry Thursday morning, my eyes felt gummy and sandy when I got out of bed, but I paid no attention to them until I caught a glimpse of myself in the bathroom mirror. I was startled to see that the whites of my eyes had turned an angry pink, and my lashes were clumped together: the distinctive signs of pink eye. I ignored my condition for as long as I could, but eventually I found myself in my eye doctor's exam room, trying not to touch my face.

How many times had I sat in this chair and counted the certificates mounted against the light wood of the walls? To someone unfamiliar with bulky eye-exam equipment, the complicated shapes might look menacing, but I'd been facing off with those machines since third grade. I cried when I first learned that I needed glasses, but the minute I put them on and discovered that I could make out a bird on a branch and every face on the playground, I loved them.

Finally my doctor breezed in. He checked my (very pink) eyes, confirmed my amateur diagnosis, and prescribed some drops. As we said goodbye, he added casually, "Make sure you schedule a regular checkup soon. As you know, you're more at risk for a detached retina."

"Wait, what?" I asked, turning around. "Actually, no, I *don't* know about that."

"You're extremely nearsighted, which makes it more likely that your retina will pull away from its normal position. It's a serious problem that could damage your vision, so if it starts we want to catch it right away." He spoke as cheerfully as if he were giving me a standard reminder to drink enough water or wear sunscreen.

"I'm sorry," I said, "can you explain that again?" I flashed back to the fact that the nurse had referred to me as a "high myope" just before the doctor came in.

He repeated himself, and I listened with mounting alarm; I had a friend who had recently lost some of his sight due to a detached retina. I became so distracted by my anxiety that as the doctor talked I could hardly hear what he was saying. (I didn't take notes, and I *always* take notes.) He finished by saying, "So I'll see you at your next checkup, okay?"

"Okay, thanks," I said, stunned, and continued out the door.

By the time I was outside, something in me had shifted. I felt frightened. My sight! Until this conversation, I had never given much thought to my sense of sight beyond making sure my contact-lens prescription was up-to-date.

As I headed home through the soft dusk, I realized that it had been a long time since I'd noticed the New York City streetscape that I loved. What if it dimmed or even vanished for me?

I turned a corner, and in an instant, all my senses seemed to sharpen. It was as if every knob in my brain had suddenly been dialed to its maximum setting of awareness. I gazed through my sticky eyes at the luminous gray sky above the buildings and at the frilly purple leaves of the ornamental kale in the tree boxes. I picked out every sound in the weekday city racket of sirens, jackhammers, horns, and shouts. I smelled a heady mixture of car exhaust, marijuana, and honey-roasted peanuts from a Nuts4Nuts cart.

Never before had I experienced the world with such intensity—it was *extraordinary*. As I continued through the streets, waves of exhilaration made me want to laugh out loud or say to a passing stranger, "Look at the trees! Aren't they beautiful?" For too long, I realized, I'd been taking it all for granted—the colors, the sounds, the feel of everything around me.

My walk home took only twenty minutes, but those twenty minutes were transcendent. I kept thinking, "This experience is *now*, it's here; and it's also *past*, never to be repeated."

In that time, I woke to a profound truth: I had my one body and its capacities right now, and I wouldn't have them forever. In college, I'd read a cheap edition of Henry James's *The Portrait of a Lady* on a top bunk with no proper reading light; now I had to enlarge my smartphone's font to answer my emails. One day I might no longer hear my husband Jamie's loud yawns, or see our dog, Barnaby, triumphantly race through the apartment with his beloved Abominable Snowman toy in his mouth. Already, our daughter Eliza was out of the apartment, and we had just a few years left with Eleanor under our roof.

I was a dutiful caretaker of my body—careful to get enough sleep, to exercise, to eat healthy food, to get my checkups and vaccines, to wear sunglasses and a seatbelt. But was I appreciating my body and its powers? Was I savoring each day of my life as it was unfolding? Was I paying attention to the people I loved?

As I pressed the keypad to let myself into our apartment building, I accepted the truth that, until now, I'd ignored: I was running out of time. Shadows had begun to slant eastward, over Central Park and over my life. I didn't want to come to the end and think, "So many things happened to me. I wish I'd been paying attention."

I came home to an empty apartment. Before long, I heard Jamie calling me from the front hallway, and I jumped up to greet him. "Hello!" I said, with a rush of love. "How was your day?" When I gave him a kiss, I noted the rough stubble on his cheek, and as we talked, I found myself gazing into his face with an intensity that let me register the green of his eyes and the gray in his dark hair as I hadn't for a long time.

I waited for Eliza and Eleanor to return from dinner with their grandparents. When they walked through the door, they seemed taller than I remembered, as though I'd looked at them without really seeing them for months.

"Hello!" I said, as I gave each of them a long hug. "Hi," they answered, with some surprise at my enthusiasm. As I pulled Eliza close, then Eleanor, I noted the scents of their different shampoos, one honey, one plum. When they were little, I'd been so physically engaged with my daughters, constantly carrying, bathing, feeding, rocking, and cuddling them. Now that they were older, I more often kept my distance. Too much time had passed since I'd held them tight.

I resolved to make a change.

MY PINK-EYE INFECTION CLEARED AFTER a few days, but I couldn't stop thinking about what I'd experienced.

For years, I'd been studying human nature and reflecting on how we can build happier lives: the science of the soul. One of my most important realizations was that we can build a happy life only on the foundation of self-knowledge. The more my life reflected my own temperament, values, and interests, the happier I became, so I spent a lot of time trying to know myself better. Before starting this process of self-examination, I'd assumed, "How difficult can it be to know myself? I hang out with myself all day long!" But self-knowledge is hard.

To know myself better, I asked myself questions: "Whom do I envy?" "What do I lie about?" "What did I do for fun when I was ten years old?" "How do I put my values into action?" I also followed dozens of happiness-boosting resolutions: "Revive a dormant friendship," "Follow the one-minute rule," "Celebrate minor holidays," and "Choose the bigger life."

Despite all these efforts, over the past few years, I'd started to realize that I felt stuck in my head—disconnected from the world and other people, and also from myself. I traveled all the way from New York City to Los Angeles to see my sister Elizabeth, but when I got back, I realized I hadn't once noticed her characteristic way of gesturing with her hands, and I had no idea if she was still wearing her signature circle necklace every day. Had I really looked at her at all?

I'd been trying to figure out what was missing from my life, and that unforgettable walk home from the eye doctor revealed the answer: *I needed to connect with my five senses.* I'd been treating my body like the car my brain was driving around town, but my body wasn't some vehicle of my soul, to be overlooked when it wasn't breaking down. My body—*through my senses*—was my essential connection to the world and to other people.

I knew, of course, that I could have a happy, complete life even if I lost some of my body's capabilities. My fear was that one day I'd regret all that I'd ignored. Today I might think, "I'm too busy to plan a trip to Death Valley," but if I lost my sense of sight, I'd think, "I wish I'd seen the desert." Some people love mountains, and others love the ocean, meadows, lakes, or forests. Maybe I loved a landscape of sand dunes, and I didn't even know it.

If I stopped to think about it, did I know the color of the inside of a blueberry? It took me years to realize how much I disliked the work of Pablo Picasso and loved the work of Thomas Cole, or that I preferred English Breakfast to Earl Grey tea. When my mother saw me wearing my favorite pair of yoga pants, she commented, "It's nice to have something navy blue, instead of more black," but I'd never registered that my yoga pants were blue. I lived in New York City, but I never spotted any famous people.

I wasn't sleepwalking through my days. I spent hours reading, writing, and talking to people; I kept lists, made plans, and set goals; I tracked the number of steps I took. I existed in a constant process of self-examination: How do I grow into the person I think I could become? But while I valued the intensity, productivity, and structure of my life, that walk home had revealed that I'd been allowing the *sensations* of my life to slip away unobserved. If I focused on the experiences of my senses, what could I discover?

I hadn't noticed when I'd started craving ginger ale or dreading the "Ripples" sound of my phone alarm. When had Eliza started wearing so many rings? When had Eleanor started blasting music while she took a shower? When had Jamie started eating so much Greek yogurt? My senses held the power to tie me to the people and moments that I wanted to experience and to remember.

That pink-eye afternoon had revealed three truths. I wanted to appreciate the moments of my life more fully; I wanted to get out of my head and into my life; I wanted to deepen my knowledge of the world, of other people—and of myself.

During that walk, I'd felt intense vitality because I'd paid such close attention to the sensations streaming through me, and that experience showed me the way forward: I would study my five senses. I didn't want to miss another minute.

I KNEW THAT THIS AIM—TO revel in my senses—wouldn't be easy for me. Many people enjoy activities that connect them to their bodies, like running, swimming, fly-fishing, or playing a musical instrument.

I read books. Petting Barnaby was the closest thing I had to a body-based hobby.

My tastes often seemed too small, too simple. I preferred plain food, like scrambled eggs at our local diner, and I couldn't handle liquor, so I rarely drank even a glass of wine. I loved the odd song, but I rarely listened to music. I wanted light massage instead of deep, I wanted my meat cooked through and my salsa mild. I admired art that seemed obviously beautiful.

I didn't make much effort to shape my experience, and I always chose convenience over pleasure. Other people went to great lengths to make the perfect cup of coffee; I used whatever system was quickest and easiest, and I swigged my coffee from a giant mug, not from a small cup that would encourage me to savor every drop. Every Christmas, we decorated artificial tabletop trees instead of a fragrant, prickly live tree. For a long time, I'd resisted my daughters' pleas to get a dog because I didn't want to deal with the extra work.

Over the years, I've had several transformative insights into happiness and human nature (I have a tendency toward epiphany, which is one of my favorite things about myself). Now I realized that, over time, I'd grown serious and impatient, too eager to hurry back to my desk or my to-do list. Although I love to work, my focus on efficiency and productivity had left me with a heaviness of spirit—a feeling of staleness or stagnation. I wanted to stir myself up with the quick hits of exuberance that my senses could provide.

My sister Elizabeth often told me, "You would have made such a good monk," and it's true. I valued my good habits so much that I almost never took a break from them, even when I probably should have. Some people lead messy lives. I wasn't messy; my faults fell in the opposite direction. I was rigid.

I could become so preoccupied with my plans and lists that I forgot to pay attention to what was actually happening around me. I'd walk on a beach but hardly see the ocean because I was rewriting a paragraph in my head. I couldn't listen to an audiobook because my own thoughts drowned out the sound of the reader's voice.

Recently, I'd taken Eliza, Eleanor, and Barnaby to a neighborhood photography shop to have their picture taken for our family's annual Valentine's Day card. I hustled the process along, trying to finish it as fast as possible so I could hurry back to my desk. Only later did I realize the irony: The whole point of taking the photograph was to capture the sight of my daughters *at that moment*—and I hardly looked at them as it was happening.

Now, perhaps, I had found a way to shake myself out of my chronic fog of preoccupation: I would undertake to see, hear, smell, taste, and touch the world around me so that instead of staying in my head, I would live more fully in my body. I would relish sensations for their own sakes, and, even more than that, I would use the intensity and emotional power of those sensations to connect me to others, and also to myself.

Coming to My Senses

I WANTED TO TAP INTO THE POWER OF MY SENSES—BUT WHAT DID I mean by "senses"?

I headed to the library to dive into research. Of the senses, I learned, five could be called the Aristotelian Senses or the Kindergarten Senses: sight, hearing, smell, taste, and touch. Our sensory organs of eyes, ears, nose, tongue, and skin are connected to the brain through nerves that transmit electrochemical messages. These organs and the brain work together to present the world to us: *Sensation* is the stimulation of a sensory organ (a tongue tasting salt) and *perception* is the integration of sensations in the brain, with all we've learned about the world (a brain perceiving "Great pretzel!" from sight, sound, smell, taste, and texture).

In recent times, however, researchers have identified many additional senses. For instance, *proprioception* gives us our sense of the position of parts of our body. We use it when we close our eyes and touch our finger to the tip of our nose or climb stairs without looking. *Equilibrioception* allows us to maintain our balance and body posture as we sit, stand, run, ride a bike, or walk a tightrope. *Interoception* gives us the ability to note and interpret sensations coming from within our own bodies. Is my heart racing? Do I have butterflies in my stomach? Am I hungry, thirsty, in need of a bathroom?

This list continues, and while every sense contributes to our experience, and is fascinating in its own right, these more subtle senses run in the background. As with a heartbeat or breathing, typically we notice them only when they break down. They don't match the glamour of the Big Five.

I decided to explore the Big Five.

The brain lives a quiet life, encased in bone and floating in cerebrospinal fluid; it's about 73 percent water and accounts for 2 percent of body weight, yet gobbles up about 20 percent of all the energy we consume. My brain allows me to accomplish extraordinary feats: Just the other day, I stood on a moving bus while reading a sign during a conversation with a friend as I ate from a bag of nuts. That's a lot of coordination.

While my eyes, ears, nose, tongue, and skin send their distinct messages along the complex circuits of my nervous system, by the time that information reaches my consciousness, it's integrated into a coherent whole. It is the *sensorium*—my sensory faculties considered together—that gives me my experience of the world.

Soon after my doctor's visit, Eleanor brought home a large container of raspberries, and I helped myself to a bowlful. I ate them one by one, captivated by their beautiful jewel-like color, their fresh flowery smell, their bumpy texture, and the explosion of sweetness when I bit into them. With effort, I could identify these separate sensations, but in the moment, my sensorium gave me pure "raspberry."

As we move through the world, our brains make constant adjustments to what we perceive. When information is incomplete, our brains make an educated guess about what we've seen, heard, smelled, tasted, or touched. For instance, because of the way the optic nerve attaches to the eyeball, we all have blind spots in our vision, but the brain typically ensures that when we look around, we don't register any gaps. When one sense doesn't give us as much information as we want, we can recruit other senses to help. If I can't track the flight of an invisible bug that is pestering me, I can listen to try to find it, because by listening to changes in sound—such as the amount of sound, how sound reflects off surfaces, and the difference in time when a sound arrives at each ear—we can learn about the location and speed of objects with our ears instead of our eyes.

Also, our five senses regularly make compromises; when one sense clamors for attention, the others fade back. When Elizabeth and I talked on the phone, my brain helped me concentrate on her words by reducing my awareness of the rain clattering against my window. When he walked into a Woolworth's store, artist Andy Warhol recalled, "I listened and there was a buzz, probably a faulty air-conditioning system, but for me it was completely drowned out by the smell of roasted peanuts."

Along the same lines, when one sense shuts down, the others feel more acute; lights dim for a concert, because we hear better in the dark; we close our eyes when kissing. I'm a fearful driver, and when I do drive, I often turn off the radio so I can see where I'm going.

In general, our senses are alert for change, because change might mean danger or opportunity. A bird's flight catches my eye, but I don't notice a rock on the ground. As soon as a sensation becomes familiar, we ignore it, so after a few moments, my skin will no longer register my cotton T-shirt, and the smell of sunscreen will fade.

In particular, each of the five senses is attuned to information about *people*. Because they're so crucial to our survival, we have an insatiable curiosity about how other people think and behave. What are they looking at, what are they saying? By watching, listening, smelling, and touching other people, we can make shrewd guesses about their identities, desires, knowledge, beliefs, and motivations. Information about other people is so compelling that it can be difficult to concentrate in the presence of others—something bemoaned by many workers who sit in open-plan offices.

The five senses send in streams of reports—yet the human world is only partly concrete. Unlike animals, we experience a universe transformed by imagination, and we exist within a cloud of thoughts, such as "What if?" and "They're talking about me" and "This is holy." A dog doesn't gaze at a waterfall. When we look, we see more than our eyes show us.

And, of course, we each live in our own body, the one assigned to us by fate and shaped by our history. My senses would show me a different world if I were ten years old, pregnant, a smoker, a bird-watcher, or in a bad mood, or if I spoke a tonal language, had a genetic variation related to the olfactory receptor gene OR6A2, or had suffered through a bad night with tequila in college. As writer Zora Neale Hurston observed, "Every man's spice-box seasons his own food."

Yet most of us assume our world is the same as everyone else's world. Remarkably, I learned, many people who have trouble differentiating red from green or who lack a sense of smell don't realize it until young adulthood. In his memoir *Songs Without Words*, Gerald Shea recounts that he was thirty-four years old before he discovered that he'd lost much of his hearing from scarlet fever, at age six. Some people with synesthesia—in which the stimulation of one sense creates an experience in a second sense so that letters or numbers have colors, music has color or movement, or words create tastes—don't know that others lack those types of impressions.

For people who have sensory processing differences, some sensations may feel overwhelming, while others barely register. Certain experiences, such as getting a haircut, walking through a crowded mall, smelling the laundry-detergent aisle in the grocery store, or feeling a sudden breeze may be difficult. These challenges require thoughtful attention and care, and different tools and strategies can help people manage their individual sensory environments.

Acknowledging that people experience sensations in different ways can help us all be more understanding—not to dismiss people's objections to sights, sounds, smells, tastes, or touches, but instead to respect them so that we can create sensory environments in which everyone can feel comfortable.

While studying such differences was beyond the scope of my project—to explore my own five senses—recognizing them underscored an important truth: We each live in the brew of our own sensations.

It was strange to realize that I make the world. In darkness and silence, my brain receives countless messages as my five senses probe my surroundings. In that outer world, there's no color, no music, no scent, until those messages return to my brain—and then the world bursts into life inside my body. "My own eyes were needed in order that the copper-red of the beech could be set against the blue of the cedar," writer and philosopher Simone de Beauvoir noted. "When I went away, the landscape fell to pieces, and no longer existed for anyone; it no longer existed at all."

When I die, certain impressions will wink out of existence forever: the prickle of dried grass underfoot in Missouri's summer heat, the bready scent of the bakery where my daughters and I stopped for after-school cupcakes, the way watery sunlight slants through my kitchen on winter afternoons.

Looking outside my window, when I noticed that snow had begun to fall, I told myself, "I don't need to look, I can look next time." No. Now, I promised myself, I would stop to experience it all. But how?

TO LIFT THE VEILS OF my self-absorption, to re-create the beautiful intensity I'd felt on that walk home from the doctor's office, I needed a plan.

Because I tend to turn personal challenges into professional projects, I'd done many self-experiments before; I'm a kind of street scientist who uses the world as my laboratory and myself as a guinea pig. I tackle questions such as "Why do we do what we do?" and "How can we become happier?" And I always start by asking these questions of *myself*.

I began to plan my investigations to go deeper into the senses. I couldn't magically outgrow myself; if I wanted to change, I must make a change. Over time, I've learned, I gain more from taking specific actions than from making lofty but vague resolutions. I wouldn't be able to prod myself to "be present in the moment," but I could "take a deep sniff of saffron" and, with its earthy-sweet scent, appreciate that moment. So how should I proceed?

Because I love habits, predictability, and familiarity, I would take a methodical approach to my experiment. I'd follow the traditional order—see, hear, smell, taste, touch—because that order felt natural to me. In humans, the visual system is the most highly developed, and next, the auditory system. Although crucial to our experience and sense of well-being, the other three senses don't dominate our awareness as much, and they occupy less real estate in the brain. It's right that smell should come before taste, because flavors arise largely from smell. The order also reflects the senses' range: Sight and hearing tell us what's happening far away; smell, at a shorter distance; taste and touch require direct contact. Touch, last on the list, is the only sense that's spread over the entire body.

For each sense, I'd begin by studying its workings. I'd been absorbing sensory reports since even before I was born, but I didn't know much about how the senses work. The more we know, the more we notice.

To engage more fully with each sense, I'd devise a mix of playful, practical exercises: take a class, plan an adventure, or try a simple experiment. I'd find ways to immerse myself in a particular sense, deprive myself of it, indulge it, hoodwink it, or cure some irritation it caused me.

I wanted to use the five senses to deepen my relationships, so I would invite my family and friends to try different exercises with me (and with Eliza and Eleanor, I'd likely conscript them). Through my senses, I hoped to find new ways to build connections with the people I loved.

Also—and this was particularly ambitious—I'd choose one place and visit it every day for a year. This exercise appealed to me because I've always been powerfully attracted to routine and repetition, and I take great pleasure in the expected. With a daily visit, I could explore what I saw, heard, smelled, tasted, and touched over time.

Some people report feeling a new shot of life after finding themselves in a dangerous situation (getting in a car crash, trying a risky adventure) or going through a demanding experience (starting a romance, having an intense encounter with nature). But I didn't want to risk my life or even overhaul my life; I wanted to transform my ordinary day. By paying more attention to the sensations I encountered, I could elevate the familiar experiences that were already part of my daily routines.

My study of the five senses wouldn't be exhaustive. I'd be studying *my* five senses, and I'd explore whatever compelled me most. Each of us comes from our own time and place; each of us engages with the world through our own particular complement of senses, whatever those might be. I could only study myself.

Even so, from my small study, I hoped to discover larger truths. I considered the staggering variety of human lives: the people who lived across the globe, the people who lived five hundred years ago, the people who lived a block from my apartment, today. All those people existed in a unique universe. I hoped that a greater understanding of my own senses would give me a deeper appreciation of the human experience.

I considered my starting point. What did I know about myself? I realized that I had *foreground* senses and *background* senses. With our foreground senses, we pay attention, we seek new experiences, we enjoy talking and learning about those senses. With our background senses, we're much less interested; we may be concerned more with avoiding the negative than with embracing the positive. While some people engage with each of their five senses, other people—such as me—appreciate some senses but neglect others.

My foreground senses were sight and smell; I tended to dismiss hearing, taste, and texture to the background. I liked looking into store windows, but I had little interest in listening to new music or trying a new food. Jamie constantly listens to new music, but he almost never comments about a smell. A friend loves to cook and try new foods, but never bothers to visit a park, store, or museum. Through this experiment, I would try to cultivate my neglected senses.

I also hoped I would discover the superpowers—for me—of each sense. Did it have a special power to evoke memories? To bring delight? To connect me with others?

These days, our five senses are blunted by sunglasses, deodorant, and shoes that cushion the sensation of gravel—and they're also glutted with high-fructose corn syrup and elevator music. When I watch a movie, I see and hear more than I could ever see or hear in real life, but no information registers in my nose or on my skin. My environment felt oversaturated and processed, but also virtual and flattened. I wanted to make direct contact.

When I talk to people about happiness, sometimes they ask, "In the midst of so much suffering and injustice, is it selfish to focus on our own individual experience and happiness?" For instance, by exploring the five senses.

My answer is: no. Research shows that happier people are interested in the problems of others and the problems of the world. They volunteer more time, donate more money, are more likely to vote, and are more likely to help others. That's why that airplane reminder to "put on your own oxygen mask before helping others" has become such a cliché; it's a cliché because it's true. When we care for ourselves, we strengthen ourselves to care for others—and I conjectured that the five senses would provide an effective way to care for ourselves.

By immersing myself in strong sensations for this experiment, I hoped I'd sharpen my five senses for the rest of my life. The days are long, but the years are short—and my years are getting shorter. As we grow older, time seems to speed up; as poet Robert Southey observed, "Live as long as you may, the first twenty years are the longest half of your life." My freshman year of high school seemed to last forever, but last year passed in a flash.

I faced not just the fragility of my physical faculties, but the transience of everything around me. I'd better enjoy every experience now, because in a blink (like this, right in the middle of a sentence) it would be gone.

Despite this weighty truth, I felt a soaring feeling of excitement every time I thought about all the things I would do. Would my five senses help me to become more observant, more creative, more loving? I couldn't wait to plunge in.

*Portrait of a Woman with
a Man at a Casement*

ca. 1440
Fra Filippo Lippi

Seeing

The Voluptuousness of Looking, or
Why No One Notices the Gorilla

The great interests of man: air and light, the joy of having a body, the
voluptuousness of looking.

—MARIO MANLIO ROSSI, "Essay on the Character of Swift"

AFTER WE BROUGHT NEWBORN ELIZA HOME FROM THE HOSPI-
tal, I remember lying on the bed with her between Jamie
and me, and thinking that I just couldn't open my eyes wide
enough, or stare long enough, to take in the sight of her.

She'd been born early, so she spent a week in the neonatal inten-
sive care unit before coming home. She weighed just four pounds,
and I marveled at her delicate features, her perfect hands: her body
so fragile, yet capable of every task of life.

I saw Jamie, too, who was fast asleep. (It had been a tough week
for all three of us.) As I looked at Eliza's carefully swaddled form
against Jamie's large and sturdy bulk, for the first time I saw him as a
father.

Eliza's face was smaller than my palm, her lashes were almost invisible, and when she opened her eyes, even though she had the inscrutable, unfocused gaze of a newborn, I felt the shock of her presence.

I'll never forget the sight of her that afternoon.

I'D WITNESSED A SUPREME MOMENT with Eliza as a newborn, but now I almost never saw the world with that kind of intensity. Every morning, Eleanor made herself two pieces of toast and sat munching them at the kitchen table while she checked her phone. Or did she?

The revelation from my trip to the eye doctor had made me realize how much I valued and depended on my sight. Something we see can make us laugh, cry, or change our lives, but too often I used my power to see in a purely utilitarian way. When I rode the subway, I relied on sight to navigate my way through the station and onto the train, but I paid little attention to the faces or fashions of my fellow passengers. "Nobody really looks at anything; it's too hard," Andy Warhol observed. It was time to learn to see.

With sight, light passes through the cornea, the pupil, and the lens to the retina, where photoreceptive cells turn light into electrical signals. These signals travel from the retina to the optic nerve to the brain, which translates the signals into images and makes meaning out of those images. Even under rapidly changing conditions, typically functioning vision systems can detect color, shape, movement, and depth. Each of our two eyes receives slightly different information, which the brain uses to create single, three-dimensional images.

I was surprised to learn that although we think we're gazing clear-eyed on the world, in fact, our brains are always tinkering with the view.

For example, *color constancy* means that we understand that a familiar object stays the same color, even when light conditions change; I know the field of snow in Central Park is white, whether I look at it in the bright sunlight of noon or in the blue light of dusk. Similarly, *size constancy* means that we understand that an object stays the same size, even when its image on our retina gets bigger or smaller; I know that tree isn't rising up out of the ground, even when it looks bigger as I walk closer to it. When I glance around the park, I seem to scan the scene smoothly, when in fact my eyes rapidly jump from one point to the next.

The brain erases things that interfere with our view, like our nose and the blood vessels in our eyes. While it gives us the impression that we see a world of crisp, clear images, actually we can see sharp details only in a small window. I stretched out my hand to an arm's length and looked at the width of my thumb—which, I'd learned, was the size of the area that I could see clearly, just enough to make out seven or eight letters of normal print on a page. Sure enough, despite this sight limitation, everything around me appeared to be in sharp focus.

Our brains combine information from all our senses, but when a conflict arises, sight usually wins. For instance, in the McGurk effect, if we see a person's mouth moving in a way that doesn't match the actual words we hear, the brain corrects our experience so we "hear" what we see.

The sight-biased wiring of our brains leads to some unfortunate trade-offs. I love beautiful smells, so I'm sorry that roses are now bred for their color, shape, vase life, and resistance to insects and disease, not for the trait that matters most to me—their fragrance. I'm not a fan of tomatoes, but I often hear tomato lovers complain that tomatoes have become colorful, tough, and bland; they're now bred for looks, uniform size, and ease of packing rather than for flavor. Sight trumps taste.

Often we miss seeing something happening right before our eyes because our brains are focused on something else. I went online to watch the astonishing Monkey Business Illusion video that illustrates "inattentional blindness." I watched six participants line up on a stage, with three wearing black T-shirts, three wearing white T-shirts. A voice instructed, "Count how many times the players wearing white pass the ball," and each team started bouncing and passing a ball. I faithfully watched the white team, and was surprised when I learned that the answer was sixteen passes—I'd caught only fifteen. Then (spoiler alert), the announcer asked, "Did you spot the gorilla?" Nope! Because I'd been tracking the ball, I'd failed to notice when someone in a gorilla costume strolled right through the action.

And this inattention doesn't just apply to gorillas. In 2019, fans of the fantasy TV show *Game of Thrones* shared a big laugh when a stray to-go coffee cup, complete with plastic lid and insulation sleeve, accidentally appeared on a castle's banquet table amid flickering candles, animal horns, and goblets. Despite many layers of scrutiny from editors, producers, and executives, no one spotted it because they were focusing on other elements as they reviewed the dailies.

While we assume that what we see, hear, smell, taste, and touch reflects the objective truth about the world, in fact, like donors in a Renaissance painting, we insert ourselves into the action; my brain shows me what it decides that I need to see. When the heel popped off a favorite shoe, I was amazed by how many tiny shoe-repair stores in my neighborhood suddenly sprang into view. My brain had decided that this information was useful.

Also, different brains come to different conclusions about how things look. The internet (and the minds of vision scientists) exploded in 2015 after a woman on Facebook posted a photo of her striped dress. The world argued about whether the dress was colored white and gold or black and blue; people just couldn't believe that anyone could see the dress differently.

I pulled up the image on my computer to look at the dress again. With most optical illusions, I could make my eyes flip between two interpretations—duck or rabbit, vase or faces—but when I looked again at that famous dress, I couldn't manage to see it as black and blue, its actual colors. I only saw white and gold. This single photograph prompted an intense flurry of research to figure out why people saw such different colors. The disagreement seemed to be due to the different assumptions a brain might make about lighting conditions. Was the dress shown in natural light, in artificial light, or in shadow? Was it lit from the front or back? Brains made different guesses.

Our sense of sight is powerful and sophisticated, but it's also fragile. While definitions of vision loss differ, more than thirty-two million American adults report being unable to see or have trouble seeing even when wearing glasses or contact lenses.

Technology—from braille to screen magnifiers and readers to GPS devices to scanners—can play a key role in helping people with vision loss to navigate the world more easily. New technologies are under development, such as "smart canes" that use ultrasonic sensors to alert users to obstacles in their path, even above chest level, and to pair with smartphones to give directions and information.

Some solutions don't depend on chips and sensors. In his thought-provoking memoir, poet Stephen Kuusisto reflects on his relationship with his Labrador guide dog, Corky:

> I'm a capable blind man who travels everywhere with a trained dog. . . . We're intuitive. Occult. We can hear everything. We think for each other. Entering the subway in Manhattan, we are a kind of centaur: man-head with dog's body . . . or is it the other way around? Maybe we have two heads. Six legs.

Sometimes we may be aware of others' different sensory worlds; sometimes not. My sister Elizabeth and I host the weekly *Happier with Gretchen Rubin* podcast, and on one episode, we interviewed journalist Frank Bruni about his experiences after a stroke damaged his sight. He pointed out that most people deal with some sort of challenge. "If we all wore sandwich boards that listed bullet points of the main things we're dealing with," he said, "all of us would be so much more empathetic, would understand where people are coming from, and would be able to connect in a way we don't." It's crucial to remember that *our* sensory world isn't *everyone's* sensory world.

Looking for What's Overlooked

To start my experiment to help my eyes explore, I set myself the task of looking for what I'd overlooked.

My brain alerted me to what it deemed important, but I wanted to train myself to spot small details, things in the background, or other sights that my eyes and brain—with all the best intentions—tried to spare me.

Since we tend to overlook the familiar, I wondered what I'd been missing. For instance, for several mornings in a row, as I made my morning coffee, I'd picked up a peanut-butter-covered spoon, rinsed it off, and put it in the dishwasher. It was only on the fourth morning that I thought to ask Jamie, "Have you been having trouble sleeping?" A spoonful of peanut butter was his favorite midnight snack, but I hadn't noticed this clue sitting on the kitchen counter; I saw the spoon without seeing it. When I knew to ask the question, Jamie told me that a difficult work problem was keeping him awake.

When the brain must process new information—when we visit a new place or try a new activity—time seems to slow down, experiences seem more vivid, and our emotional responses are more intense. That's why a week on vacation seems longer and more memorable than a month at home. On the other hand, when we follow routines and every day looks the same, our experience speeds and blurs. One afternoon, I walked to the mailbox at the end of my street to mail a letter and then returned home. After I'd been home for an hour, I wasn't sure if I'd mailed the letter or not, because every aspect of that little errand had been so unremarkable.

It was clear that I was overlooking a lot. And so during my daily walk with Barnaby, instead of getting lost in my thoughts, I pushed myself to *look* around me. I gave myself assignments: Look for the color purple, or at trees, or at hats. I studied the materials of the different apartment buildings. One building was made of dark red-brown brick, the next of white brick, the next of yellowish smooth stone slabs. I'd walked these blocks hundreds of times, and I'd never noticed the mismatch before. (And yet the awnings were all dark green. Why? In other neighborhoods, awnings came in many different colors.) When I paid attention to dogs, I saw puppies who raced at the ends of their leashes and old dogs who had to be coaxed along; some dogs were friendly while others ambled past, indifferent. So many dogs were outfitted with booties or coats—should we be allowing Barnaby to run around naked?

The more I looked, the stronger the habit grew. I found more beauty—in the surprising orange tweed of a woman's coat, in a flock of birds wheeling overhead—and I also found more whimsy. As I walked down city streets or grocery-store aisles, I found playful examples of hidden images.

Some of my favorite discoveries:

I spotted the hidden arrow between the *E* and the *x* on the FedEx trucks that I saw so often.

In the aisles of my grocery store, I discovered the hidden chocolate kiss between the *k* and the *i* on a bag of Hershey's Kisses, as well as the happy chip-eating people on a bag of Tostitos.

I knew that some people called Baskin-Robbins "31 Flavors," but I never saw the "31" incorporated into the logo until Eliza pointed it out as we walked together down Lexington Avenue.

I'd recently been seized with the desire to learn to play poker, so I'd been spending a lot of time with cards in my hands. And for the first time I saw the hidden white "8."

For a different exercise to help me see what I'd overlooked, I recruited Eleanor to help me take a "forced perspective" photograph. In this type of optical illusion, objects are photographed from a vantage point to make them appear bigger, smaller, closer, or farther away to create funny effects. For instance, years before, in a classic tourist move, I'd taken a photo of Eliza that seemed to show her pushing against the Leaning Tower of Pisa.

One Sunday afternoon, Eleanor and I headed to Central Park, where we made our way to the ancient Egyptian obelisk that stands

on a hill behind the Metropolitan Museum of Art. I wanted her to take a photo that created the illusion that I was balancing the monument on my palm.

"This feels so dopey," I told her as she positioned me. "I wish the park weren't so busy!" I had to keep stepping aside for people walking by with their strollers and dogs, who watched my poses with mild, tolerant curiosity.

"Well, you do look a little silly," Eleanor said. Later, though, I heard her telling a friend about what we'd done and making plans with her to repeat our experiment.

That afternoon forever changed the way I saw that area of Central Park. I'd walked through it dozens of times, but I'd never noticed the slope of the hills, the placement of the trees, the way the obelisk stood against the sky—and now I did. My afternoon with Eleanor made me see the world differently.

See something once—really *see* it—and it never looks the same again.

However, despite my efforts, I was still overlooking some of my most familiar and important sights. I went to a men's clothing store to buy Jamie a present, but when I got there, I had no idea what to buy. "Does your husband wear sweaters?" a helpful clerk asked.

"Well, you know," I said with some embarrassment, "I'm not sure." *Did* he wear sweaters? I knew he *had* sweaters—I could picture them on a shelf—but did he wear them?

"He loves jackets," I offered. That, I knew. Jamie loves jackets. He didn't buy much, but he did love to buy a jacket.

"Terrific," the clerk said. "What does he need? Something lightweight?" He gestured to one side of the store. "Or something heavier, or waterproof?"

"Yes . . . great questions," I said. I had no idea what he already owned. Day after day, he'd pulled on those jackets, and I couldn't remember a single one.

Later, when I was home, I looked hard at Jamie as he sat filling out a crossword puzzle. When had he switched to a digital watch? And no, he wasn't wearing a sweater.

He glanced up and caught me staring at him. "What?" he asked.

"I'm just looking at you."

"Why?" he asked with a laugh. "Stop it!"

Jamie was so important to me that I hardly bothered to notice him. I needed to change that.

Gazing at Faces

The more I learned, the more I realized how much our brains, our sight, and our other senses are particularly attuned to one category: *other people*. Human survival has always depended on our ability to cooperate, and we're among the most social species on the planet. Other people represent both safety and danger, so the brain and five senses search relentlessly for information about those around us.

Because people are so important, we love to gaze at faces. "The goal of all art is the human face," said the artist Paul Cézanne, and the brain devotes tremendous power to processing faces. This attention makes sense, because from faces, we learn so much. The face is an identifier: We can recognize hundreds and perhaps thousands of different individuals, from different angles—which is remarkable, given that faces, really, are very much alike. The face is also an information dashboard that gives us insight into other people's pain, pleasure, interest, and attention.

According to Roman statesman and writer Cicero, King Xerxes the Great "offered a prize for the man who could invent a new pleasure." *Inventing a new pleasure* seems like an impossible task, yet this explains the extraordinary attraction of YouTube, Snapchat, TikTok, Instagram, and, of course, *Face*book. They give us entirely fresh ways to gratify our desire to look at faces. We can view more faces in a single scroll through social media than during a lifetime in a medieval village.

To represent people, we use faces. I read that when three-year-olds are asked to draw a person, they draw a face with legs, so I decided to check Eliza's and Eleanor's handiwork. I dug through the trove of school art that I'd carefully preserved—and to my astonishment, I saw that each of them drew exactly that way (although Eleanor also added stick arms). The sight of their drawings, so careful and expressive, made me wistful.

Eliza:

Eleanor:

Any facelike pattern may activate the brain's fusiform face area, the part of the visual system that specializes in facial recognition, and our brains look for faces so eagerly that they sometimes see faces where they don't exist. This phenomenon of *pareidolia* explains why we see the Man in the Moon or the face of the Virgin Mary on a grilled cheese sandwich (which, by the way, sold for $28,000). I looked around my office for hidden "faces," and I immediately spotted this pair, with their anxious "Oh, dear!" expressions.

Typically, when we look at faces, we focus on other people's eyes. Of the body, the face is the person; of the face, the eyes are the person. Eyes reveal identity, so to mask people's identities in photos, we put a bar over their eyes. Eyes demonstrate awareness: In an "eye-opening ceremony" for a painted or sculpted image of the Buddha, the eyes are painted last, to bring the image to spiritual life.

Eyes can provide clues into what other people are thinking; gaze can reveal curiosity, suggest a thought, or make a connection. Recently, Jamie and I walked into a loud party, and I spotted someone I knew Jamie would be happy to see. I caught Jamie's gaze, smiled, briefly glanced across the room, then looked back at Jamie. He followed my gaze, then nodded. Without a word, we had a conversation.

Eyes may also help us signal that we're ready to speak, that we're listening, or that it's time for others to take a turn. Teachers tell students, "All eyes on me," because eyes drive attention.

Because it's so powerful, for many people, eye contact can cause great discomfort. This intensity also perhaps explains why some celebrities resist eye contact. Katy Perry, Tori Spelling, Luke Perry, and

Sylvester Stallone are just a few examples of figures who reportedly have made this request of the people around them.

At a conference I attended, the event's leader told audience members to turn to a stranger and hold eye contact for fifteen seconds, then talk about why they'd come to the event. I was surprised by how *intimate* this exercise felt. In ordinary life, I would never hold eye contact with a stranger for so long—those fifteen seconds seemed interminable. (Some research suggests that after about four seconds, people begin to feel awkward.) Despite my discomfort, however, the exercise did give me a distinct feeling of connection.

Back home, I tried the eye-contact exercise again with Jamie, and we did it for thirty seconds. That time felt uncomfortably long, but the fact that we could sustain that long gaze underscored our bond.

Learning more about eye contact convinced me to improve my behavior on video calls. Rather than looking into other people's eyes on the screen, which had been my habit, I worked hard to train myself to look into the camera. That way, I appeared to be making eye contact.

The problem? If the people on my screen also wanted to appear to make eye contact, *they* had to look at *their* cameras. Which meant that by trying to create the impression of eye-to-eye contact, we had to look away from each other's faces altogether—which would weaken our sense of connection.

Eyes command attention.

Making the Daily Visit

For my five-senses investigation, my most ambitious experiment was my plan to visit one place every day for a year. By returning to the same place, week after week, and by learning what I could see, hear, smell, taste, and touch there, I hoped that I'd learn more about both the place I visited and myself.

For me, doing something every day was easier than doing it "whenever I felt like it" or "some days." If daily, this visit would become part of the architecture of my life and would remind me each day to focus on my senses.

Surprise stimulates the brain, and research shows that people who do new things and visit new places—even something as modest as a trip to a new restaurant—tend to be happier. Nevertheless, I think that the pleasure of doing the same thing, every day, shouldn't be discounted. I agree with writer Gertrude Stein: "Anything one does every day is important and imposing." I love repetition. Doing the same thing over and over makes me feel grounded in my life and makes my actions feel more meaningful.

So I needed to find a place that I could visit easily, day after day. A large place, an interesting place—an inexhaustible place. I decided on the Metropolitan Museum of Art.

Standing along the edge of Central Park in Manhattan, the Met is one of the world's largest art museums. In an imposing building big enough to house eight soccer fields, it holds vast collections of paintings, sculptures, and decorative arts, as well as musical instruments, costumes, and armor. Some objects were made five thousand years ago; others, last year.

I'll never forget my first visit to the Met, in college. I don't remember anything else about that trip. Was it my first time in New York City? Was I alone? How long did I stay? All I remember is my determination to see for myself all the objects from one of my favorite novels from childhood, E. L. Konigsburg's masterpiece, *From the Mixed-Up Files of Mrs. Basil E. Frankweiler*. In it, eleven-year-old Claudia and her nine-year-old brother, Jamie, run away from their Connecticut suburb to spend a week living in the Met. They sleep in an elegant but musty sixteenth-century bed, scoop up their spending money from a fountain, and even solve a mystery. To me as a child, their adventure seemed glamorous and exciting, and yet also like something that I might be able to pull off myself.

On my first visit, I'd raced around to find the bed that Claudia and Jamie slept in, the sarcophagus where they hid their school belongings, and the bronze cat who shared Claudia's smug expression. I felt such joy at finding the real-life versions of objects that had lived so long in my imagination. (It's always reading that makes me want to experience things.)

Those days, I lived within walking distance of the museum, but I didn't visit it nearly enough. I'd go with family or friends when there was a particularly interesting exhibit, or if someone was visiting from out of town, but I never went by myself and just *looked*. If I moved away, I knew I'd reproach myself: "Why didn't I go to the Met more often?"

When I told my college roommate about my experiment, she said dryly, "Note to self: Move within walking distance of the Metropolitan Museum." Point taken. I lived within walking distance of the Met, and I had the time and the freedom to visit. I was *extremely fortunate* to be able even to attempt such a plan. But here's the thing: I'd lived near the Met for years. The fact that I could visit was no guarantee that I would visit. The museum had always been there, waiting, but I'd mostly ignored it. No longer.

Another bonus of my daily visit? I'd be walking.

The brain—like the rest of the body—benefits from movement. Walking sharpens long-term memory, reasoning, concentration, and creativity; sitting is better for focused problem-solving. I've had many of my best writing ideas while on my feet, so I was glad to have a sensory challenge that required daily movement. (I was surprised to learn that it's the walking itself that's considered the main factor, so I'd get the same boost on a treadmill in an empty room. *But would it be the same?* I doubted it.)

Before I started, I drew up the rules for my Met Experiment— I do like rules and structure. For my daily visit:

- To support the museum, I would join as a member, even though I, like all New York State residents, could visit absolutely free.

- When the Met was open, and I was in New York City, I'd visit every day.
- My visit could be long or short.
- I'd explore every gallery, stairwell, hallway, café, and gift shop, as well as the exterior of the museum.
- I'd pay attention to the objects, and also to all the sensory aspects of the experience.
- I could wander aimlessly or I could set myself an objective—whatever I felt like doing on a particular day.

During law school, I spent so much time in the library that I learned every inch of it; it was where I did my work, wasted time with my friends, stored my stuff, and even where I met Jamie (our carrels were back-to-back). It came to feel more homelike than my dorm room. I wanted to make the Met feel like mine as well.

As I was getting ready to start this experiment, I met a friend for coffee, and when I mentioned my plan, her face lit up. "That's a great idea," she said. "I'd love to come with you sometime. I was a summer intern at the Met during high school, and I go back every chance I get."

"So here's my question," I said. "To me, the Met seems inexhaustible. What do you think: If I do this for a year, will I reach the end?"

She shook her head. "You'll never reach the end." This promise of limitless exploration thrilled me.

I'd assumed that my desire to visit the same place every day was fairly idiosyncratic, but when I posted online about my plan, I was surprised to hear that many people were already making their own daily visit, or wanted to do it—to a nearby beach, horse barn, community garden, hiking trail, even a castle.

We are serial expatriates and I've had places like this everywhere I've lived. In Seoul, we lived a short walk away from the National Museum of Korea, which was surrounded by gorgeous traditional gardens.

I visit where my son is every day. He was 34 and lived with us. I was his full-time caretaker. It is a small rural cemetery, and we put a bench there where I can sit. It is a lovely spot. I feel close to him there.

Wonderful to return to the same place over and over again and find new things and have new experiences each time. My places are a nearby reservoir and my local CVS drugstore where I enjoy chatting with some of the regular workers.

I find great peace and inspiration in spending a little time every day in a church or chapel.

For me, as for many people, a new year is a particularly auspicious time to start a new project. Because I was away on a family trip for the New Year's Day holiday, I first headed to the museum on January 4, a bright, cold, fresh day. I climbed the Met's majestic steps with the sense of excitement and possibility that I'd felt on the first day of school each year.

Once inside the inviting warmth of the Great Hall, I paused to unwind a brown knitted scarf from around my neck. My ears rang with the cacophony of visitors' polyglot chatter as they bought their tickets. I'd hurried through this grand space many times, but I'd never before looked up to see its monumental limestone arches and imposing domes, and I'd never looked down to appreciate its mosaic floor in white and gold marble—this time I couldn't resist crouching to slide my fingers across its cool surface. The hall featured four columns on each side and an eight-sided information desk anchoring the room's center, and it was bright with sunshine that poured in from round skylights and huge windows.

Research shows that the design of spaces influences our thinking. High ceilings stimulate expansive and abstract thoughts; symmetry pleases our sense of balance and vitality; spaces rich with symbols, layers of meaning, and interesting designs help us to think. In a neighborhood crammed with interchangeable Starbucks coffee shops, the Met was grand, distinctive, and awe-inspiring.

As I walked through the space, I was surrounded by people—some poring over maps of the museum, some studying the banners that indicated where to find various galleries, others chatting in small groups as they waited for some straggler to appear. To my surprise, I discovered a colossal statue of a seated pharaoh looming above the milling tourists. Just as I'd missed the gorilla who sauntered through the players passing balls, I'd missed this ten-foot-high royal figure, right in the center of the Great Hall, on all my previous visits.

This time, with my new focus on sight, I managed not to overlook it. Composed, full of strength, and made of dark stone, the ancient figure of a divine ruler made a sharp contrast to the colorful, jittery bustle of the crowd. I walked over to study the hieroglyphics carved into the throne. I recognized the ankh, the Egyptian symbol for life, and I could pick out pictures of birds and cattle. Maybe the museum would teach me about hieroglyphics.

My daily visit was under way.

Collecting Color

As time passed, and I made my daily visits to the Met, I took particular pleasure in admiring the colors on display. I made it a point to walk past the glowing red rose in Horace Pippin's *Lady of the Lake* or to appreciate the rich yellow-orange amber of a Chinese porcelain vase.

A few years ago, I'd become intensely interested in the subject of color. Because I have to read about something in order to see it clearly, I read everything I could about color—and it turns out that there's an astonishing volume of literature about color.

Color seems like a steady, objective feature of the world while, in fact, color blinks in and out of existence. Color enters the body when light radiates off an object and is absorbed by photoreceptor cells in the eyes, and the eyes send signals to the brain, which deciphers the message as color. Without an object, without light, without an eye, without a brain, there's no color. It vanishes every time we walk out of a room or night falls. "Color slips through the fingers and escapes," director Derek Jarman wrote. "You can't lock it in a jewel box as it vanishes in the dark."

It may be elusive, but color isn't a frivolous, decorative aspect of our experience. Color vision helps us perform the important visual tasks of perceiving forms, shapes, textures, depth, motion, and contours. Color gives us insight in sight; it informs us while it delights us.

Although we all encounter the same spectrum of visible light, different languages have greater or fewer basic color terms. Using the English language, I describe color in eleven basic shades: blue, yellow, green, red, orange, pink, purple, brown, and the paradoxically named "achromatic colors" of black, white, and gray. By contrast, the Berinmo language spoken by people of Papua New Guinea has five basic color terms, while the Tsimané language spoken by people of Bolivia has three. Different languages name colors differently; for example, the Russian language has separate terms for "light blue" and "dark blue."

Despite people's fascination with color codes, colors have no inherent meaning or universal effects. Blue isn't calming, red isn't energizing, and painting a jail cell "drunk tank pink" neither reduces aggression nor suppresses appetite. We supply meanings to color from our own time, place, culture, and private associations.

For instance, today in the West, pink suggests "girl" and blue suggests "boy," but before World War II, pink was a boy's color, because red was a martial color, and light blue, with its association with innocence, purity, and daintiness, was a girl's color. In the United States, green is associated with healing and nature; across the Muslim world, green is associated with Muhammad—it was said to be his favorite color—and for that reason appears in the flags of many countries.

Even within a single culture, a color doesn't have one specific meaning. Where I live, red is the color of love and hell, protection and danger, violence and joy. Black is used for sexy lingerie as well as mourning clothes; it's the color of the plain and the luxurious.

And yet, despite the fact that it has no fixed meaning, color moves us in very specific ways. We see beauty or ugliness, we feel comforted or unsettled, we feel warmer or colder, as soon as we see color. A friend told me, "When I see a color that's just right, I *feel* it in my body, I get a physical rush from it. It can change my mood." I knew exactly what she meant.

Every day, as I walked outside in the season of deep winter, nature offered gray, brown, dingy green, and pale blue, one of my least favorite color combinations. I could hardly imagine that in a few months, clusters of yellow daffodils would blossom in the park's refurbished spring landscape of fresh green, deep blue, and delicate pink.

I craved ways to satisfy my wintertime hunger for brilliant color. One of my happiness-project resolutions is to "indulge in a modest splurge." As shallow as it sounds, sometimes I could boost my happiness by buying something that I didn't absolutely need but that made my day brighter in some way.

On a visit to an office-supply store, I spotted a set of felt-tip pens in bright, unusual colors. I love any set of colored markers, which, like a color wheel or fan deck of paint colors, embodies color in its purest form. This set of pens was the perfect modest splurge—why write with boring black and blue when I could use olive green, fuchsia, caramel brown? Purchasing those pens gave me the same pleasure that I'd felt as a child when I got a new box of crayons.

I brought the pens home and put them in my favorite pen cup, and every time I used one, I noted its unusual color. My favorite was oxblood; I love colors that hover on the cusp of other colors, and oxblood manages to look purple, brown, and red all at once. Beautiful tools make work a joy, and these pens gave me a boost of happiness every time I held one in my hand.

Also, I began to note how people added a splurge of color to their appearance; clothes and cosmetics are among the artistic expressions of everyday life. In a packed airport waiting area, a staid-looking man had paired his black pants and charcoal sweater with canary-yellow socks, and the woman standing next to him displayed one of my favorite color combinations with her cherry-red necklace against a deep maroon shirt. Many people enjoy wearing nail polish as an easy way to add color to their everyday life. Because Eleanor loved to paint and repaint her nails, the next time I was in a drugstore, I picked out two colors—magenta and forest green—to bring home to her.

Noticing all these rich colors inspired me. I wanted to *create* something out of color.

I've always loved the sight of many different objects united by a single hue. Years ago, I saw a photo of Portia Munson's *Pink Project*—thousands of cheap pink objects arranged on a table—and I'd never forgotten it. Munson's artwork reminded me of an idea proposed by Diana Vreeland in one of her extravagant *Harper's Bazaar* columns:

> *Why Don't You* . . . have a room done up in every color green? This will take months, years, to collect, but it will be delightful— a mélange of plants, green glass, green porcelains, and furniture covered in sad greens, gay greens, clear, faded, and poison greens?

Thinking of Munson and Vreeland, I was inspired to create my own collection of objects of the same color. This project appealed to me for two reasons. First, I've always enjoyed a hunt. As a child, I loved finding a penny on the ground, doing word-search puzzles, and poring over every detail in Richard Scarry's *Best Word Book Ever*. As an adult, I loved spotting a favorite title on a library shelf, but other than that, I didn't have many opportunities to exercise my love of the hunt. Here was my chance.

Also, I wanted to create a mass of color out of objects. I have friends who arranged their books by the colors on the books' spines, and their color-blocked shelves looked terrific. When objects share one color, there's no clash, only beauty.

But what color?

In my study of human nature, I often posed questions to people such as "Are you a marathoner or a sprinter?" and "Do you love simplicity or abundance?" When I asked people, "Do you have a signature color?" I was astounded by the enthusiasm of their responses. People are passionate about color.

I couldn't commit to a single signature color for myself—I fudged my answer by choosing the "color wheel"—but I could select one color to collect. I chose a deep, luxurious red that was popular but not too popular, had extravagant associations, and was also a beautiful word to say: *scarlet.*

I'd go on a search for scarlet and build a collection of scarlet objects. I pulled out a big glass bowl—a wedding gift that we never used—to fill with the items I found.

As one of our family traditions, Eleanor and I often went on after-school "adventures" together. Usually this adventure wasn't particularly adventurous; we might visit a museum or an unusual shop. Lately, though, Eleanor hadn't been very enthusiastic about our outings. On the one hand, I didn't want to miss this time with her, when it was just the two of us with no tasks or distractions; on the other hand, this excursion was supposed to be fun, not an obligation.

Eleanor had, however, become very enthusiastic about going to thrift stores. (Teenagers often develop a love of thrift stores, the way fifty-year-olds develop a love of gardening or surfing.)

"For our weekly adventures," I suggested to Eleanor, "why don't we visit a different thrift store, in a different part of the city? And I'm on a search for scarlet, so we can look for scarlet items to add to my collection."

"I would *love* that!" Eleanor said. "That would really be fun."

The very next week, we headed to our first thrift store: Unique Boutique on the Upper West Side. The weather was icy, so we hurried from the crosstown bus stop into the store. We stepped into a classic thrift shop: circular racks of clothes, shelves of unwanted DVDs, a collection of books that ranged from blockbuster bestsellers to the obscure, and rows of household goods. Its walls were covered with art for sale, and I'm partial to thrift-store art.

As I scanned the shelves, I admired a set of heavy white ceramic salt and pepper shakers shaped like cookbooks, then a set of plates patterned with old-fashioned nosegays and ribbons. Nothing scarlet, however. But even though I hadn't found what I was looking for, a quest is more fun than a jaunt.

Eleanor hurried across the store to show me something she'd unearthed. "How about this for your collection? It's scarlet." She held up a small, plastic fire truck in brilliant red.

"You found something! Perfect!" I said. "How much is it?"

She turned it over to find the price tag. "One dollar."

"Sold."

She held up a necklace with wooden beads. "Can I get this for myself? It's six dollars."

"Absolutely."

Over many visits, as my collection slowly grew, I realized that it gratified my magpie instinct. It was harder to find these items than I expected, and I enjoyed a rush of satisfaction whenever I pounced on some small scarlet item. I didn't always find something to buy, but I always enjoyed the hunt. Considered one by one, none of these objects was interesting, but just by being the same color, the group became remarkable.

My search for scarlet helped me look harder—and when I looked for color, I saw things in a way that I hadn't seen them before. Wherever I spotted "my" color, I felt a thrill of recognition. In a coffee shop, I saw a man wearing a scarf of a pure, deep scarlet, and I was tempted to compliment him on his choice. Another morning, in snowy Central Park, I noted a cardinal's red feathers glowing against the brilliant white of the landscape. A cardinal in the snow is surely one of the most hackneyed examples of the pleasures of sight, true, but this was the first cardinal I'd noticed in years.

More important, my search had deepened my relationship with Eleanor. Considered separately, these little mother-daughter adventures were quite forgettable, but tied together by my search for scarlet, these hours stood out, and I could remember them far more vividly. The search made our time feel *purposeful;* I was searching for scarlet, she was hunting for clothes, and we were enjoying our time together.

Immersing Myself in Sight

I felt the urge to overwhelm my sense of sight with spectacle—at the Met, at a thrift store, and everywhere else. Clearly I wasn't the only one who craved this kind of extreme sensory encounter, because I kept seeing experiences promoted as "immersive."

One afternoon, I headed downtown to Pier 36 to visit the popular traveling exhibit *Immersive Van Gogh.* (I had to double-check my information to make sure I was going to the right place; to my amusement, an unaffiliated exhibit called *Van Gogh: The Immersive Experience* was also on view nearby.)

I handed over my ticket and walked through three cavernous, interconnected rooms displaying two-story-high images of Van Gogh's work, in projections that repeated across every wall and onto the floor. Each enormous room was empty, except for some chairs and some large silvered blobby statues that reflected the walls in an interesting way. The overall effect was overwhelming.

I sat cross-legged on the floor to watch as a stream of animated images—a greatest-hits sequence of Van Gogh paintings—emerged, floated, and dissolved. The flames of painted candles burned, the wings of insects flickered, clouds and water moved, flowers blossomed, olive trees burst into view and faded.

The magnification changed the experience of viewing Van Gogh's work. His characteristic brushstrokes were easier to see, but they were flattened and expanded, like dough under a rolling pin. Similarly, the scale distorted the usual proportions of his work; a bouquet of flowers was ten feet tall.

The "immersiveness" came from the size and repetition of these projections. Music played throughout, which both heightened the emotional force of the pictures and—because it discouraged talking—kept the audience's focus on the display. I was so preoccupied by my sense of sight, however, that I noticed sounds only when I reminded myself to pay attention to them.

I understood the appeal of this way of looking. It was a thought-provoking and unconventional way to view an artist's work. And, because the exhibition was purely visual, it could be enjoyed by people of any age, for any length of time; it required no preparation or previous expertise (or even, really, any interest in art). It was an experience, a visual extravaganza.

While this kind of show might help us see Van Gogh's work with fresh intensity, I wondered if it might also cause us to crave images that shimmered and moved. (That's a common concern, of course: that by amplifying sensations, technology will spoil "natural" experiences.) When I thought of Van Gogh's work in the Met, the contrast made those paintings seem smaller, static, plain. I wanted to use technology to take me deeper into explorations of sensations, but I didn't want technology to commandeer or coarsen my senses.

On my next visit to the Met, I headed to the galleries that held the Van Gogh paintings and studied one of my favorites, *Self-Portrait with a Straw Hat*. While the images in *Immersive Van Gogh* had covered giant walls, this painting was the size of two cereal boxes. I decided that while viewing those maximized, animated displays had helped me to note brushstrokes, color juxtapositions, and small details that I'd previously overlooked, it hadn't displaced my love of standing in front of the actual painting—the thing itself.

Asking How to See

A few weeks later, as I headed into the new Second Avenue subway station at Ninety-sixth Street, I paused to admire the blue-and-white murals on its porcelain-tiled walls. They depicted sheets of paper swirling in a sudden gust of wind, and these images caught the feelings of energy and possibility that often hit me when I walk through a subway station.

By chance, I knew the person who'd created this work, the artist Sarah Sze. We'd met in college and reconnected years later, when our daughters were in the same fifth-grade class. As I took in the immense installation she'd created, the thought struck me: *Hey, I could talk to Sarah about how to see better. Maybe she could help alter my perspective.*

Sarah was game, so one Monday afternoon we met in the lobby of the Met. After we'd caught up for a few minutes, Sarah offered, "I have a few ideas for pieces that would be interesting to look at."

"Okay, let's go," I said. "That would be great."

We headed up the monumental stairs into the Baroque Portraiture gallery. There, we stood in front of Orazio Borgianni's *Self Portrait as a Painter with Palette and Canvas,* which shows the artist sitting, chin in hand, with his palette nearby.

"With this one," Sarah said, "so much is about the act of seeing."

"How so?" I asked.

"The artist is painting a self-portrait," she answered. "He's looking at himself in a mirror, so even though he's looking out, he's looking at himself, not us. We can't see his painting—only its back." She pointed to the right side of the picture, which, I now noticed, showed the unfinished side of a canvas. "We see him using the very paints that he used for this painting." I looked at it and felt a deep surge of satisfaction as I *saw* the painting become richer.

"It's a conversation across time," said Sarah.

As we walked to another gallery, I asked Sarah for suggestions to help the eye to see. She had several ideas: Look at an artwork in a hand mirror, to see it reduced and reversed; print out an image, to place the artwork in a different context; squint at it, so details vanish to reveal the larger composition; and hold up a hand to block one part of the work, to see how that absence affects everything else.

As we walked, Georges de La Tour's *The Penitent Magdalen* caught Sarah's attention. "Look at how much of this painting is in darkness. The *restraint,* the silence." She stood in front of it, looking.

I'd seen that painting many times, but Sarah showed me things I'd never noticed before—how Mary Magdalen's unbound hair hung past her waist, how the light from a single candle illuminated her pale bare neck. When I'd looked at the painting in the past, I'd understood that the jewelry abandoned on the table and floor symbolized Mary Magdalen's rejection of worldly pleasures, but I hadn't realized that perhaps La Tour was drawing attention to her neck to suggest that we were witnessing the very moment of her renunciation.

As we moved through the galleries, the instant Sarah's eye fell on an object, she wanted to look more closely. As we talked, I tried to take notes.

"Every color changes every other color."

"You have to look at what's left empty."

"Scale shifts are very important. I learned this from Asian landscapes."

"Where something enters and exits a painting is very significant."

"With art, you want to create the unexpected. Being forced to get oriented helps people to stop and see."

As we walked through the Modern and Contemporary Art mezzanine, I pointed to Kerry James Marshall's *Untitled (Studio)* and told Sarah, "I really love this painting."

"Oh yes," she said. We stopped in front of the artwork, which shows an artist's studio crowded with people, canvases, and a worktable covered with jars of brushes, paint cans, a vase with flowers, an anatomical skull. "Yes. This painting is about the very act of seeing, of making art." She started pointing out details that I'd seen—but never considered. "We see the work of the studio, with the backdrop, the lighting, the canvas, the nude model waiting."

The longer we stood there, the more she pointed out. "Look at the skull, that's such a traditional object for art. And look, it has an eyeball."

"Sight!" I said. Nothing could more directly symbolize the sense of sight than an eyeball popping out from a skull.

"And look at the plane of the canvas, and the plane of the backdrop; the red color shows their relationship. He's painting air," Sarah added with admiration. "That's so hard."

The more we looked at the painting, the more beautiful it grew, and the more remote.

She turned to me to say, "Now show me something else you love."

"Great!" I led us across the length of the museum to the greywacke sculpture *God Horus Protecting King Nectanebo II* on its high pedestal. I never tired of gazing at its pure lines.

"Oh, I love this sculpture," Sarah said. "I've looked at it many times."

I felt pleased with myself for making a good choice. "What do you love about it?"

"It really holds the corner of the room, and it's displayed at the proper height. As humans, we orient ourselves to the human figure, which is placed at eye level, and the god towers above us and envelops us. Look at the feet of the pharaoh nested within the feet of the divine."

"Right," I said. I noted the shift in scale she'd talked about earlier. "A pharaoh is always depicted as far bigger than other people, so the tiny pharaoh shows the majesty of the god."

"And look how still it is, silent, and absolutely grounded and symmetrical." We stood, looking.

It was almost time for the museum to close, and as we walked toward the front doors, I couldn't resist pointing out another favorite nearby. It was a small, round reddish-brown bowl that rested on a pair of sturdy, bare human feet. The bowl was tipped forward, as if it were politely offering its contents.

"I love this little bowl," I said. "It has so much personality."

"It's so great," Sarah replied. "This shows how we connect through time. You're seeing this, and the person who made it is seeing you. That person thought this thing was humorous, and you think so, too."

"Do you think that the artist found it humorous?" I asked. "I wondered if, maybe, to my modern eye it's funny, but the artist didn't intend it that way."

"Oh sure," Sarah said with confidence. "Look at the way the feet turn in. This was meant to be funny. And it was made in"—she checked the label—"about 3700 B.C."

Finally, we looked at Perneb's Tomb, an installation of an actual Egyptian tomb. I'd walked by this structure many times, without much interest.

"I love this," Sarah said. "It brings everything together—painting, sculpture, architecture." As we talked about it, I began to appreciate the stately lines of the heavy stone and the details of the hieroglyphics lining the walls.

"All art is actually about death," Sarah said, "but not in a bad way. We're standing in front of a tomb, and the whole museum is a tomb. It's evidence of us being human on Earth; what it means to be alive."

All art is about death, but not in a bad way. I would ponder that.

Just then a museum guard interrupted us. "The museum is closing," he said, pointing behind us. "Please continue to the exit."

It was time to go.

Shaping What I See

As a thank-you gift for a favor, a colleague sent Jamie a large orchid. I set it on the chest by our front door and found myself pausing every time I walked past it. The orchid's wide petals glowed with a pattern of deep and light fuchsia streaked with white, with a bright yellow-orange throat, all set off brilliantly against the green of its leaves. The color pattern reminded me of the breathtaking color combinations of traditional Japanese kimonos; I could hardly tear my eyes away.

This simple pot of flowers added so much beauty to our apartment that it got me thinking: What other easy efforts could I make to shape my sensory experiences? I realized that I could tackle this aim from both directions—by adding *good* or removing *bad*. I could add something beautiful, like an orchid, or I could eliminate an eyesore or distraction.

First, I looked for ways to add pleasing sights. One challenge was that I was an "under-buyer." Why buy flowers? They just fade and die. Why light candles? They just burn away. Now I pushed myself to indulge in a few modest splurges, to add beauty. For instance, to replace the makeshift container I'd been using to store my office supplies, I bought a large, sturdy box, covered in a pleasing pattern of white flecked with gold, that looked much nicer on the shelf.

In many cases, I didn't have to buy anything new to add beauty; I just needed to make some small effort. Instead of plopping a bag of clementines onto the kitchen counter, I put the clementines in a glass bowl and placed the bowl in the center of the kitchen table. Much better.

However, noticing more beauty also meant noticing more mess, and I found that removing unpleasant sights did even more to lift my spirits than adding pleasant ones.

Years ago I'd learned that for me, outer order contributed to inner calm, and I made a lot of effort to keep my surroundings organized and clutter-free. As I started paying more attention to what I was seeing, however, I noticed that I'd allowed piles of to-be-read books to accumulate on various surfaces.

I decided to eliminate this eyesore. The easiest solution was to move these books out of sight. But where and how would I store them?

After roaming around the apartment, I saw that I could repurpose a set of wire shelves that stood outside my office door. With some effort, I cleared some big items out of a closet to create room, carried in the wire shelves, and arranged my books in neat horizontal stacks. In the closet, the books looked nice, and the other rooms looked much better without them.

When Jamie came home from work, he paused and slowly looked around him. "It looks good in here," he said. "What's different?"

"I put my stacks of books in the closet, to get them out of the way."

"They were blocking the light from the window," he said. "It really makes a difference."

This new arrangement cured two irritations. First, when I removed the unsightly stacks, the room instantly looked more open and inviting. Second, now that the books were collected and arranged attractively, I enjoyed visiting the closet to survey the shelves.

Inspired, I looked for another quick victory.

My smartphone screen was a jumble that I confronted dozens of times each day, so I took a few minutes to clean it up. I deleted the apps I didn't use, created more folders like "Travel" and "Photo and Video," and moved my most-used apps to the home screen. Relief.

After I'd cleaned up my home screen, I sat for a moment and considered my phone. I was tempted to blame it for my disconnection from my five senses. More than just about anything else, this device had the power to distract me from my concrete experience, with its dazzling show of colorful photos, stories, and information.

I once saw a guy so transfixed by his phone that he stepped off the curb and walked straight into three lanes of oncoming traffic. He kept going, despite the fact that I, and several other people, started yelling. He looked up only when a car screeched to a halt in front of him. I was so shaken by the sight of this near catastrophe that I thought I might throw up, but the man, after stopping for a moment, continued to the sidewalk, still looking at his phone.

I've never walked into a busy street (yet), but I've certainly spent a lot of time tethered to a screen. People have always worried about the effects of new technologies: Writing would destroy our memories, electric lights would ruin our eyes, speeding trains would damage our brains. In our time, we worry about smartphones, email, social media, video games, and the internet, and it's absolutely true that these newfangled attractions ceaselessly clamor for our attention, with more captivation optimization with every update.

And yet while I must master technology, more important is that I must master myself. To assert myself over my smartphone, I figured out how to switch my screen settings to the "grayscale" display limited to black, white, and gray. Without the enticements of color, I predicted, I'd be more likely to put down my phone.

My prediction came true immediately. As soon as I made the change, I started to use my phone far less. In black and white, it felt more utilitarian and less playful. Social media sites and my own photos were far less compelling. I had to work harder to locate my apps, and when I was browsing online, it was hard to find specific links when I didn't have color to help me navigate. I'd use my phone to do a specific task—to check my email or to answer a text—but instead of jumping to other distractions, I'd put it down.

Also, to my surprise, after a few days, the colors around me started looking brighter; apparently, my frequent glances at the glowing, hyper-vivid images on my phone had made the real world seem dim by comparison. I recalled what Sarah had told me: "Every color changes every other color."

"What's wrong with your phone?" a friend asked after she happened to glance over my shoulder.

"I put it in grayscale mode, so colors don't show up."

"Can I look at it?" She studied my home screen. "Do you like this? It's so ugly."

"That's why I did it. It's a lot easier to keep off my phone when it's like watching some old black-and-white TV set."

"Maybe I should try it," she said, handing it back. "Is it hard to switch?"

"No, it's simple." I showed her how to change her settings. "Also, you have little kids. Grayscale makes a device a lot less fun."

"Genius."

After a few days of grayscale, I switched my phone back to full color. Wow! I'd forgotten how much color added to the smartphone experience. Deprivation is an effective way to reawaken ourselves to a sensation; sometimes, we enjoy something more when we enjoy it less.

I preferred to use my phone in full color—but I could switch back anytime I felt too spellbound by its glowing screen. More generally, I'd learned an important lesson: Instead of passively accepting the scenery of my life, I could find ways to shape my sensory environment to include more beautiful eyefuls and fewer eyesores.

Seeing More

As the winter days passed, I realized that my five-senses experiment was having an effect: I was seeing the world more clearly, I was noticing more.

When I met a friend for coffee, I paid attention to her retro style. When I put on makeup, I noticed how the pink powder shimmered in its compact and how my pale eyelashes popped into view as I brushed on dark mascara. As I walked through the apartment, I loved catching sight of my collection of scarlet items, glowing in their glass bowl. Although I'd seen Jamie do it hundreds of times, I really noticed his daily habit of sizing himself up after he got dressed: He stood in front of the mirror, squared his shoulders, then patted his chest a few times as if to say, "Okay, ready for action."

Why bother to look at Jamie when I see him day after day? Because the day may come when I'll think, *I would give anything to gaze into his face one more time.* I didn't want the people most important to me to fade into the background wallpaper of my existence; sharpening my sight sharpened my appreciation of what I loved most.

In the Met, *looking* led to *noticing* led to *appreciating*. For instance, initially I wasn't much interested in ancient Greek and Roman art, which I thought of as "heads without bodies and bodies without heads" (plus all those indistinguishable black-and-red vases). Once I looked more closely, however, particular objects caught my attention. For one thing, those disembodied heads showed a wide variety of elaborate hairstyles. According to their labels, various heads boasted "closely cropped curls," "tousled curls," "corkscrew curls," and even "snail-like curls." The museum's fashion-magazine descriptions struck me as peculiar until one label informed me that because aristocrats' hairstyles changed often and were well documented, coiffure offers a significant clue in dating objects. Who knew?

Similarly, as I looked more closely at case after case of similar Greek black- and red-figure vases, I began to spot distinctions. By learning what to expect, I gained the chance to be surprised. For instance, on one vase, instead of the usual soldiers, horses, or gods enacting their divine business, two women struck an astonishingly casual, modern pose. As they listened to a seated lyre player, one woman stood behind the other with her chin digging into her companion's shoulder—exactly the way my daughters sometimes stand together. The familiarity of that informal posture suddenly made ancient times feel much closer. When I really stopped to *look,* the world was far more interesting.

I was surprised to realize that, for me, one of sight's superpowers was its ability to help me connect with other people. Eleanor and I teamed up to take a funny photo, and we browsed together in thrift stores. I visited the Met with an old friend. Now I understood why people so often meet to visit a historical monument, natural wonder, shopping mall, open-house tour, or planetarium, or for some other visual adventure. Tapping into our sense of sight is a way to share an experience; it brings the world into the conversation.

I connected with Eliza through sight even when we weren't in the same place. Eliza and I had a tradition that whenever we went to the Met together, we visited a medieval stained-glass window to look at our favorite toothy cow, goofily grinning down at baby Jesus.

Now whenever I spotted that cow, I texted a photo to Eliza. I never added any words but just used the image to tell her, "This is where I am, and I'm thinking of you." She usually answered with a heart emoji. As quick as it was, this wordless exchange of images brought us closer.

My frequent visits—and my new attention to the overlooked—also fed my imagination. Not unlike an author who has carefully edited every word of a book but uses boilerplate for the copyright page, the Met lavished attention on certain areas of its building but neglected its stairwells, restrooms, and escalators. I kept thinking, "Something great should be happening here. This is the *Metropolitan Museum*." I entertained myself by dreaming up ways to make these fringe areas more interesting. (One idea: Place a violin case and a book bag in some out-of-the-way corner, to be discovered by fans of *From the Mixed-Up Files*.)

This, I realized, was a superpower of sight for me: When I looked around while letting my thoughts drift, I put myself in a state of unfocused attention that both calmed me and ignited my creativity.

When I told Elizabeth about my attempts to *see* everything around me instead of wandering around in a fog, she asked, "Is it some kind of walking meditation?"

"I don't think so," I said. "With meditation you're supposed to be intentional with your thoughts. I just let my mind off the leash. I walk around, look around, and think about whatever I think about. It might be meditative, but it's not meditation—maybe it's the *opposite* of meditation."

"That sounds more appealing than meditating," she said. "Also easier."

"Yes," I answered. "I think so, too."

Ngoma (drum)

19th century
Vili or Yombe people

Hearing

◎ 〰 ⟨⟩ ⬦ ⋀

Snow on Water, or How Silence Can Be Noisy

Snow on water: silence upon silence.
—Jules Renard, *Journal*

T HE OTHER DAY, AS I WAS WALKING ACROSS A MARBLE FLOOR IN high-heeled shoes, the sound triggered two memories simultaneously, from very different parts of my life.

I remembered being seven years old and trying on a pair of patent-leather shoes in Swanson's, a department store in Kansas City. I loved any chance to visit the children's floor, which had a colorful painted wooden tree that spread its branches low over the aisles. Once I'd put on the shoes, my mother told me to walk around to see if they fit properly, and as I walked across the hard floor, the tapping sounds of those shoes made me feel very grown-up.

And another memory flashed up, from years later. I was rushing around our apartment in New York, doing last-minute preparations for a surprise birthday party that my mother, sister, and I were throwing for my father. Earlier in the day, I'd picked up a flower arrangement, and as I hurried from one room to another, my heels clicking against the floor, I heard four-year-old Eliza say softly to her babysitter, "My mommy is having a flower party"—and I was overwhelmed with the astonishing realization that *I* was the mommy, *I* was having a flower party.

Now, once again, I heard the soft clicks of my shoes.

OUR HEARING ANCHORS US IN the world; it tells us what's happening behind us, above us, in the dark, and before we're born.

Sound pumps me up, calms me down, and transforms my moods in just a few seconds. My hearing can wake me from a sound sleep and lull me back into a doze (as I'd recently experienced when I awoke to the unwelcome sound of Barnaby throwing up on the carpet, then listened to a podcast to help me fall back asleep after I'd cleaned up the mess and crawled back into bed).

As I learned more, I became increasingly astonished by the extraordinary sensitivity and sophistication of human hearing. We can detect a vast range of sounds, determine the direction from which a sound comes, and screen out noises so we can pick out what interests us.

In typical function, our outer, middle, and inner ears work together to turn vibrations in the air into signals to be interpreted by the brain. Our hearing depends on two factors: frequency and intensity. Frequency—whether a sound is low or high—is measured in hertz, and the human range starts at about 20 hertz (low rumbling sound) and goes up to 20,000 hertz (high-pitched squeak). Intensity, or loudness, is measured in decibels, and the human range starts at 0 decibels (leaves rustling is about 20 decibels), and anything louder than 85 decibels (busy city traffic) can threaten our hearing if we're exposed to it over time. Because our two ears are on either side of our head, they receive different information, and this difference helps us to locate the source of a sound.

Humans—and many other animals—have a predisposition to interpret a sudden, loud sound as a warning and a long, quiet sound as calming or neutral. We understand the difference between a bird's alarm call and a cat's purr.

Hearing gives us valuable information. One evening, as I was getting ready to push my way through a subway turnstile, I heard two men yelling. I paused to listen. The voices came from around a corner, so I relied on my hearing to tell me whether I was overhearing a dangerous fight or a friendly disagreement, and whether the men were nearby or on the other side of the tracks. My ears told me what I needed to know: Two passionate Knicks fans were arguing about basketball, just out of sight.

To experiment with hearing, I headed to the internet, to the amusing "Virtual Barber Shop." I put on headphones, closed my eyes, and listened. I was entertained by the illusion of scissors, hair clippers, and people moving around my head. Next, I listened to the Shepard tone, in which a sound seems to go impossibly higher, higher, higher, when in fact it's the same eight complex tones on repeat. (It's the audio equivalent of watching the stripes rise on a barbershop pole, or looking at M. C. Escher's *Waterfall* drawing.)

Different ears hear different sounds. One factor is age; children tend to have more sensitive hearing than adults. Another factor is the language that we speak; for instance, people who speak a language that doesn't distinguish between *r* and *l* find it difficult to hear a difference between "red" and "led."

Just as people see "the dress" as white-and-gold or black-and-blue, in the famous acoustically ambiguous "Laurel or Yanny" audio clip, about half of listeners hear a voice say "Laurel" while half hear "Yanny." I heard "Laurel," without question, and it was hard to believe that anyone might hear something else. People hear different words depending on their sensitivity to higher and lower frequencies and on acoustic context.

Just as we're always *looking* for other people, we're always *listen-*

ing for them, too. Particular areas of the brain selectively pick out and activate at the sound of the human voice. From birth, we prefer sounds that are like speech, and, in the brain, vocal sounds generate more activity than nonvocal sounds.

And just as people's faces give us a wealth of information, so do their voices. We recognize hundreds of voices, and with people we know well, we recognize their voices after just a few words and can hear whether they're in a good or bad mood or in good or bad health. Even with strangers, from a brief listen, we can make good guesses about a speaker's age, health, education, background, personality, and social status; we can often tell if that person is tired, drunk, or sick. From the first moment she says "Hello" on the phone, I know whether my mother wants to ask a question, report an interesting piece of hometown news, or just catch up.

Sometimes we don't even need to hear a voice to make an identification. I drink a lot of Diet Coke, and years ago, as Eleanor napped in her crib, I was tiptoeing past the closed door of her room when I thoughtlessly cracked open a can of soda. It made that distinctive pop. *"Mommy?"* Eleanor called out in a hopeful voice. Busted.

We communicate through sound with our voices—and also with our laughter. Laughter is a universal, nonverbal emotional expression through sound, and we laugh long before we can speak. Although across the world people may laugh at different things, we can recognize the sounds of laughter from others, no matter what culture they're from, even though laughter can take the form of snorts, grunts, gasps, wheezes, or squeaks.

The main purpose of laughter is to bind people together; it's a social sound that's meant to be heard by others, to create engagement. We're far more likely to laugh when we're with other people, and when we're with friends rather than with strangers.

Warm, shared laughter signals a playful intent and a wish to connect. It strengthens relationships, breaks tension, makes people feel included, and helps us cope together with challenging situations.

Laughter can make us happier, and it can also make us healthier. It stimulates the heart, lungs, and muscles; cools down the stress response; helps us stay alert; improves the immune function; and relieves pain.

Sadly, however, laughter can also be an instrument of ridicule, humiliation, and exclusion, when, instead of laughing with people, we laugh at them. This kind of laughter is also social: It often comes from a desire to force people to conform or to isolate them from a group.

Laughter is so important that when we can't supply the sound of actual laughter, we fake it. For decades, TV shows added laugh tracks of recorded laughter to their programs; because laughter is contagious, hearing those artificial laughs made the audience laugh more. Today, we find ways to convey silent laughter over our smartphones. As of 2021, the laughing-so-hard-I'm-crying was the world's most popular emoji, and we write "lol" or "haha" and add funny GIFs to connect through laughter.

We spend a lot of time listening to ourselves as we laugh, talk, and sing, but we hear those sounds inaccurately. When we speak, we hear our voice through our ears, and we also pick up vibrations in the skull made by the vocal cords—which makes our voice sound richer and deeper. When we hear our voice coming from somewhere else, it sounds higher and thinner, which is why so many people dislike hearing recordings of themselves.

With hearing, as with all our senses, we perceive what our brains decide we need to perceive. They strip out what's too familiar to bring to our attention and help us focus on what's most interesting. When Jamie starts talking to me while I'm watching TV, I easily tune out the conversation on the screen in order to listen to him.

While I understood how this sifting process worked, I was always surprised when I actually confronted it in my own life. A journalist came to my apartment for an interview, and during the recording, she suddenly stopped, hit Pause, and said, "Let's wait until that's over."

"Until what's over?" I asked, puzzled.

"The siren," she said. "You don't hear it?"

I cocked my head, then nodded. "Now I hear it." A siren sound in New York is so common that my brain doesn't bother to alert me.

"It's funny," she said. "In New York City, people never hear sirens. In Los Angeles, it's helicopters."

When I'd started my five-senses exploration, I'd known that hearing was one of my neglected senses. Although I depended on my sense of hearing, I didn't particularly rejoice in it. I didn't pay enough attention to sound to be able to identify a symphony by Mozart, a birdcall by a mourning dove, or a song by Beyoncé. I might note a fight in the subway, but I made little effort to shape my sound environment.

Hearing offered me a great opportunity for more pleasure, if I could pull it into the foreground. How could I listen more closely to the sounds around me and to the people I loved? How could I embrace the beauty of silence? There must be a way.

Creating an Audio Apothecary

If I wanted to pay more attention to my sound environment, music seemed like the obvious place to begin.

All human societies have music, and music plays an important role in activities as varied as dancing, physical work, military exercises, and religious observances. While we don't all use the same scales—musicians in sub-Saharan Africa, in the Middle East, in China, make different, distinctive choices—we all know what sounds like music to our ears. Researchers puzzle over why a practice that's unnecessary for survival is nevertheless pervasive. Perhaps it's related to our use of language, or our need to come into rhythm with other people, or our desire to find a mate or build a community.

Whatever its evolutionary explanation, studies prove what everyone knows: Music has a dramatic influence on our bodies, our minds, and our behavior. For instance, listening to music during medical procedures can lower a patient's heart rate, blood pressure, and anxiety level, and music can help people to manage pain. And, just as music helps patients, it can help doctors: Surgeons listen to music in the operating room to help them stay focused and relaxed. Research shows that listening to music during exercise boosts performance and makes exertion seem less strenuous.

Music improves our health, and it also makes us feel good. There's a reason we talk about "sex, drugs, and rock & roll"; hearing a favorite song stimulates the same brain chemicals as drugs, sex, and good food. That's why it is one of the quickest ways to get a mood boost and relief from stress.

In general, our brains search for patterns and breaks in pattern, which can help us make useful predictions: If I know that shiny surfaces can be slippery, I'll walk carefully on an icy path. This interest in pattern and surprise gives us our love of both familiarity and novelty. When we experience something familiar—a song, a favorite snack, an episode of *The Office*—our brains process it more easily, which may make us like it more. Nevertheless, to enjoy ourselves, we usually try something new. Novelty is more work but also more interesting, which is why new forms of music, art, and fashion catch our attention.

Music appeals to our attraction to both pattern and surprise. When listening to a new song, we may anticipate the next note with pleasure, then be thrilled when the music violates our expectations.

The tension between the appeal of familiarity and the restless drive for novelty propels music's evolution. When the Beatles exploded in popularity in the 1960s, some listeners found their insistent beats disturbing; today, familiarity makes the same songs seem light and fun. But even if music is always evolving, we are not: Throughout our lives, we tend to listen to the kind of music we listened to when we were twenty or younger, because that's when our musical taste was established. If we're older than twenty-five when a new form of music appears—as hip-hop did in the late 1970s—we probably won't enjoy it much.

While music is an ancient and universal source of human pleasure, I almost never chose to listen to music from *any* era—not when I was with friends, walking around, in a car, or going about my day. (Put it this way: My smartphone music collection held only thirty-six songs.) When Eleanor or Jamie played music in the kitchen, I'd often instinctively turn it off. I never went to concerts, never sang in the shower, never talked about music.

Recently, when I'd gone in for an MRI scan, the technician seemed taken aback when I turned down his offer of music.

"Really?" he asked. "Most people want music."

"No, thanks," I answered. For me, more sound would've made the procedure more stressful, not less.

Now I wanted to tap into this powerful source of happiness, but I wasn't sure where to begin. Should I listen to the Great American Songbook? Choose a performer and immerse myself? Learn to play the ukulele? Then I got an unexpected insight from my friend Chuck Reed, who was the executive producer of the *Happier with Gretchen Rubin* podcast and had worked with musicians for decades.

One day, while waiting to start a recording, I asked, "How did you happen to start working in sound?"

"Through music," Chuck replied. "I've loved music my whole life. I remember listening to my mother and uncle playing their guitars in the kitchen—their voices and instruments harmonizing. It gave me such a feeling of elation."

"Because you're so aware of music and sound," I asked, "do you notice sounds that other people don't pick up?"

"Yes! Like when I listen to a podcast, one person will sound louder than the other, and I can't stand that. Also," he added, "some airplanes changed their flight paths, so now they cross over our neighborhood. I'm leading the fight to get that stopped, but I have neighbors who don't even *notice*."

"Does sound make you happier?"

"Absolutely. Like I love listening to music in the kitchen. My wife loves music, too—she's a singer, she's done musical theater. So we always play music while we're cooking or barbecuing."

"Hearing you talk about music makes me wish I appreciated music more myself," I said, feeling wistful. "I don't have much of an ear for music."

"You say that, but I think you *do* have an ear for music," Chuck said. "More than you think, just in your own way."

"Really?" I was surprised. "Why?"

"So many stories you've told in your *Little Happier* episodes have been about a powerful response you had to a song."

I was interested in music? I'd never thought of myself that way. But for the first time, instead of belittling my response to music, I tried to understand it.

Chuck was right: Music did give me strong emotions. I choked up when I listened to "The Farmer and the Cowman" from the musical *Oklahoma!* or to Nina Simone singing "Feeling Good." So what was different about the way I responded to music?

Well, I knew, many people liked to listen to an entire genre of music, or to all the music of their favorite artists, or to the radio, or to personalized playlists. They listened to lots of music, and they were always on the hunt for new music.

Not me.

Chuck's observation showed me a truth about myself: I loved *specific songs*. Most people were *musician-focused* or *genre-focused*; I was *song-focused*. If I happened to hear a song I loved, I would listen to it over and over, but I wouldn't follow up to listen to other music by that particular artist or in that genre.

Sometimes, I loved a song the minute I heard it—but not very often. More often, I became familiar with a song by accident and over time grew to love it. For instance, because Eliza likes Joanna Newsom, she went through a period of constantly playing "'81." The first time I heard the song, I asked, "What the heck *is* this?" I listened as an ethereal voice, with little accompaniment, sang a melody that veered unexpectedly. It sounded like nothing I'd ever heard before.

"It's Joanna Newsom. She's playing a harp." Eliza started singing along.

"I can't believe you can sing this," I said. "This music is so strange, my brain can't even process what's happening." And then after I'd heard "'81" several times, I suddenly loved it and listened to it over and over. (Without any desire to listen to other Joanna Newsom songs.)

I'd always felt inadequate in my response to music, and because my way of discovering and loving music didn't feel like the "right" way—too simple, too small—I ignored it. But there was no right way or wrong way. To get more pleasure from music, I realized, I didn't need to change; I needed to accept my song-by-song way of loving music.

Once I embraced my way of listening, I started enjoying music far more. When I heard a song I loved, I immediately added it to my smartphone's playlist. I allowed myself to enjoy that *one song*. Be Gretchen.

Many songs on my growing playlist put me in a wistful mood—which I appreciated sometimes, but not always. I knew from both research and everyday experience that listening to an upbeat song was an easy way to get a quick hit of energy and cheer, so I decided to create an Audio Apothecary, a special playlist of songs that gave me a boost.

For inspiration, I went to YouTube to listen to Dolly Parton singing "Mule Skinner Blues." It made me so happy to hear this cheerful, yodeling song—*hey, hey!* That song was my first addition to my Audio Apothecary. Over time, I added more songs:

"You're Dead," Norma Tanega
"You Really Got Me," The Kinks
"Pon de Replay," Rihanna

"Not Fade Away," Buddy Holly & the Crickets
"Shiny Happy People," R.E.M.
"I've Got a Feeling," The Beatles
"These Boots Are Made for Walking," Nancy Sinatra
"Hey Ya!" Outkast
"I Want You," Savage Garden
"Good Vibrations," The Beach Boys
"Push It," Salt-N-Pepa
"Feel It Still," Portugal. The Man
"Rhapsody in Blue," George Gershwin (it's the final two
    minutes that I love—it's a song with a big ending)

As I added to my Audio Apothecary, I didn't allow myself to worry about what my choices revealed about me. I dismissed thoughts like, "Would someone else think this song is sentimental?" or "Is this song cool?" If it made me happy, I put it on the playlist, so creating my Audio Apothecary gave me a new way to know myself and what I enjoy. Also, because every song reminded me of the time when I'd first grown to love it, my playlist made me feel more connected to my past: to the feeling of getting dressed to go to a party during college, or driving to the beach a few summers ago.

Over the years, I've learned that it's important that we give ourselves treats—which may sound self-indulgent or frivolous, but it's not. When we give more to ourselves, we can ask more from ourselves. Treats help us to stick to challenging goals, resist unhealthy temptations, and shrug off small irritations. When we don't get any treats, we can begin to feel burned-out, depleted, and resentful.

For this reason, I was always on the hunt for treats, and with my Audio Apothecary, I'd created a new one. Listening to one of those songs gave me a hit of dopamine, as if I'd won a bet or bitten into a chocolate bar. Even better, I could indulge in music as much as I wanted. I wanted treats, yes, but I didn't want to give myself something to feel *better* that ended up making me feel *worse*. Music was a healthy treat.

Just as my search for scarlet had helped me to see more, my search for songs helped me to hear more—and enjoy music more. Whether I was in a friend's apartment, at the drugstore, or watching TV, I listened more intently to music because I was always on the alert for new songs to add to my Audio Apothecary.

When Chuck said, "I think you *do* have an ear for music, just in your own way," he helped me see myself in a different light, to recognize a new truth about myself.

Attending a Concert

Realizing that my style of music appreciation was song-focused—rather than musician- or genre-focused—explained why I didn't have much desire to go to concerts or to buy albums.

Why would I listen to hours of Beethoven when I just wanted to listen to the first three minutes of Symphony no. 7 in A Major, op. 92, second movement, Allegretto? Why would I go to a Kate Bush concert when I just wanted to hear "L'Amour Looks Something Like You"?

Nevertheless, a musical performance is one of the oldest and most popular ways to enjoy the senses, and with my new ear for sound and music, I wanted to try listening at a concert. But what concert—and how did people know about concerts? My brain assumed I wasn't interested, so it never flagged this information for me. Should I head to a stadium, an indie coffeehouse, a formal concert hall?

I stumbled across an item that intrigued me: Among the many listings on its crowded calendar, the Manhattan venue Feinstein's/54 Below offered *Sondheim Unplugged*, which featured the songs of the revered composer-lyricist Stephen Sondheim. In this decade-long series, I read, various Broadway and cabaret performers sing Sondheim accompanied only by piano. I also learned that Feinstein's/54 Below was a "Broadway Supper Club." In other words, the audience would eat, drink, and listen to music.

I was intrigued by the prospect of a Sondheim concert because everyone in my family loves Sondheim. Eliza told me that, when she was little, she thought Sondheim's name was Stephen "Songtime"— which, if true, would have been an excellent example of nominative determinism. But my own knowledge of Sondheim was very shallow, and I'd never seen some of his biggest shows, like *Sweeney Todd*, *Company*, or *A Funny Thing Happened on the Way to the Forum*.

I was persuaded, so I bought tickets for Jamie and me. Jamie was usually the one who made plans, so I was pleased that I'd arranged a fun evening for once. But when the day of the show rolled around, Jamie said, "Don't be mad, but I'm not going to be able to go tonight."

"*What?* Why not?" I asked.

"We're reaching a deadline. We need to get six people on a call, and tonight is the only time that everyone can do it. I really have to participate."

"Are you *sure?*"

"Yeah," he said. "I'm sorry."

"That's too bad!" I said, disappointed. "I'll miss you—plus it's 'cabaret seating,' so I'll be sitting with other people. Which might be awkward."

"I really am sorry," he said, and pulled me into a hug.

A few hours later, I headed to the Theater District and walked down steep steps into the belowground club on Fifty-fourth Street (hence the name "54 Below"). The interior was filled with tables and banquettes arranged around a low, broad stage with a piano. It felt intimate.

After a waiter led me to my seat, I discovered that I was indeed sharing a four-top banquette table with two men who were already settled in. I'd brought a book, but this arrangement made it impossible for us to politely ignore one another.

"I'm really sorry," I said as I slid into my seat, "but my companion can't come tonight, so I'm crashing your conversation."

"That's okay. Don't worry about it!" they said together. In a gesture that was truly welcoming, the man sitting closer to me moved to the center so that instead of sitting two against one, we became a group of three.

My tablemates turned out to be great company. Peter and Charlie were two old friends who had started out in New York City at the same time. Then, years ago, Charlie had moved to Dallas with his wife; Peter still lived in Brooklyn. Because Charlie was in town for work and they both loved Sondheim, they'd decided to come to this concert.

Over drinks and dinner, we talked about Sondheim, the five senses, old-time radio plays, and movies.

No sooner had we finished eating than the lights dimmed, a master of ceremonies took the stage to introduce the opening number, and five performers gathered to perform a song I knew: "Sunday" from *Sunday in the Park with George*. Appropriately, given that I'd come to this concert as part of my five-senses mission, the song was about painter George Seurat's struggle to capture the colors, light, and images of an ordinary Sunday.

Next, a woman took the microphone to sing "Send In the Clowns." When I'd mentioned to my father that I was coming to this concert, he told me that he remembered the very first time he'd heard that Sondheim song.

"When you heard it, did you think, *Wow, this is a classic song that people will know for years?*" I asked.

"No," he said, "I didn't think *that*. But I do remember hearing it, and that's unusual."

Between numbers, the "host" introduced the songs and provided context and theater lore about Sondheim and his work. Quickly the songs became less familiar to me, and I'm sure I would have appreciated the music more if, like many people in the audience, I'd spent countless hours listening to *Follies, A Little Night Music,* and *Gypsy* and knew the words to every song. Nevertheless, I enjoyed the opportunity to listen. Was there a song to add to my Audio Apothecary? Sondheim's lyrics are famous for their complex ideas and pleasing rhymes, so I paid close attention to the words—something I rarely did when I listened to music.

Because these songs weren't being projected across a big theater, the performances sounded more tender and revealing. I could feel the emotions build through the audience as we listened together to the meditative "No One Is Alone" from *Into the Woods* and to the rueful, triumphant "Being Alive" from *Company.* At one point, the evening's host told a story of when Sondheim himself had sat in this room—"Right *there!*" he said, pointing dramatically to me. I felt a thrill of connection.

The concert lasted about seventy-five minutes, and the evening made me happy from start to finish. Because this kind of experience was so rare for me, it was more intense. I had enjoyed talking with two strangers, and I had enjoyed listening with them. Most of all, I was made happy by the range of sentiment I'd experienced: Through Sondheim's music, in one evening I had felt more emotion, more deeply, than I usually would have felt in a week.

The next day, as I put on Barnaby's harness to take him for his morning walk, I sang out to Jamie, "Barnaby/needs to pee/probably/ Don't I sound/Sondheim-y?"

"Sure," he said with a smile.

Bathing in Sound

As I'd learned from the Sondheim concert, enthusiasm spurs us to adventure. Whether it's tennis, gardening, Thai cuisine, or speaking Italian, a passion gives us a reason to go to a new place and talk to new people.

One person's enthusiasm can spark curiosity in others. My sister

Elizabeth loves a "sound bath," an immersive experience where, to promote calm and healing, participants listen to sounds. These sounds might be created by bells, gongs, or, most often, singing bowls, which are metal or crystal bowls struck by mallets to create rich, resonant tones. "Sound baths are really popular here in L.A.," Elizabeth told me. "I think they're more relaxing than a massage."

I wanted to try this sound-focused experience for myself. Conveniently, knowing my interest in the sense of hearing, a friend forwarded me a link to a sound-bath meditation. "Thanks!" I responded. "I just signed up. Want to join me?"

"Sure!" she wrote back.

A few weeks later, I headed to the Flatiron District to meet my friend at Fotografiska, the New York location of a Swedish photography museum housed in a historic building. I thought that a museum was an odd place for a sound bath, but, I learned, Fotografiska hosted many nonphotography programs.

We walked through the gift shop on the first floor to take the elevator up to a big open room with brick walls, wood floors, large windows, and a huge image of a flickering candle projected onto a screen. Ten yoga mats fanned out from a set of several white crystal bowls, so we sat down on two mats and waited.

"What exactly happens?" she asked in a low voice. "I've never been to one of these before."

"Me neither," I answered. "All I know is . . . *sound*."

After a brief greeting, the instructor led us and eight other participants through a few stretches and short meditation exercises. Then we lay down on yoga mats. With a mallet covered with a suede-like fabric, she began to strike the bowls or circle their outer edge to produce a sustained note.

The bowls created sounds that were unusually clear and pleasing, without discernible patterns. I could understand why singing bowls were associated with meditation, because these sounds and their reverberations did seem more *soulful* than most sounds.

As I listened, I reflected that while I could play a "sound bath" on YouTube, most of the power of this experience came from the fact that the sound was happening *in this moment, in this place.* If I weren't paying attention, I'd miss it. No recording could replace it. I could hear vibrations in the air, and also through the floor on which I lay.

Also, all my senses were working together to create this moment: I was listening to sounds, and if I opened my eyes, I saw the candle video on the screen and the instructor moving among the bowls; I caught the occasional scent of floor cleaner and the fresh, cold air from the drafty windows; I felt the squishiness of the yoga mat and the presence of other people.

But soon, I stopped having these kinds of thoughts. I wasn't aware of the time passing, and while I'd expected that forty minutes might feel like a long time, I had no feeling of boredom or impatience. I felt as though I had sunk to the depths of the ocean.

When it did end, I asked my friend as we scrambled to our feet, "What did you think? How do you feel?"

"Relaxed, maybe?" she said, with a slightly skeptical air. "How about you?"

"It was interesting. Very calming," I answered.

We walked out the door and onto the sidewalk. "Want to get coffee or something?" I asked.

"I'd love to, but I can't," she said. "I'm meeting my husband for dinner. It's our anniversary."

We chatted for a few minutes, then I headed to the subway. As I reflected on the sound-bath experience, I realized that it had allowed me to experience the pure pleasure of one of my senses—hearing—with no thoughts like *Do I like this song?* or *What happens next?* There was no pattern to discern or judge, no curiosity to satisfy, no information to process, no need to respond. With computers, phones, and books battling for my attention, this pure engagement of my hearing made me feel grounded in my body.

Also, I'd enjoyed the chance to do something with a friend that was out of the ordinary. We'd had a reason to meet and we'd shared a new sensory experience. But the next time I planned this kind of adventure, I'd make sure that we allowed time to talk about it afterward.

Taking the Microphone

Because of the delicate structure of the ear, our hearing is vulnerable to damage. We're born with about sixteen thousand of the cochlear hair cells that allow us to pick up sounds, and these cells don't regenerate. If they're harmed beyond repair—for instance, by loud sounds that persist too long—hearing is lost.

About 37.5 million American adults report some issue with their hearing, which can be a consequence of exposure to loud noise, heredity, head injury, disease, health conditions, medication, or, most commonly, age (almost half of people over the age of seventy-five have difficulty hearing).

For those who want it, different forms of technology can serve to supplement sensation. Hearing aids amplify sound and can help filter out background noise, and users themselves can move the devices in and out of the ear canal (I was surprised to learn that ordinary wireless earbuds like AirPods can be used as hearing aids). By contrast, cochlear implants require surgery and work by directly stimulating the auditory nerve.

A few years ago, my father became one of the 7.5 million Americans aged sixty or older who wear hearing aids. He'd expected that his large, stiff fingers would make it hard to manipulate the devices, so he was pleased to discover that he could easily manage them.

"What did you notice when you started wearing hearing aids?" I asked.

"There were so many little sounds that I hadn't known I was

missing, like the rustling of the newspaper when I turned the page, or coffee pouring," he told me. "And I realized how high I'd turned up the volume on the TV."

When we recognize that people's sensory experiences may differ, we're better able to show consideration. As just one small example, an event organizer once told me, "Always take a microphone. Speakers sometimes insist that they don't need it, that they can speak loudly enough to be heard. But always use the mic."

"I understand why people don't want one," I said. "Sometimes, it seems more down-to-earth to talk without it."

"You might assume that, but it's actually very thoughtless," he said. "Even if some people say they can hear you, other people might not hear as well. Amplification makes a big difference."

Not long after that conversation, I interviewed a friend at a bookstore event for his new memoir. As we settled ourselves onto stools at the front of the audience, the organizer said, "It's a pretty small room. Do you want to deal with microphones, or would you rather just speak up?"

"What do you think?" my friend asked me.

"Absolutely, let's use the microphones," I said. Now if I'm offered a microphone, I take it.

Some people, of course, don't depend on sound for communication at all. Renowned French actress Emmanuelle Laborit, who was born without a sense of hearing, recalled her first glimpse of people using "beautiful and mesmerizing" sign language when she was seven years old:

> I don't have a precise recollection of that first, stupefying visit to Vincennes when I watched in awe as all those hands whirled about. . . . I just remember my astonishment at seeing my father understand what Alfredo's hands and Bill's mouth were saying. At the time, I still didn't know that because of those men I was going to acquire a language.

After I read Nyle DiMarco's memoir, *Deaf Utopia,* Elizabeth and I interviewed him for the *Happier* podcast. He won *America's Next Top Model* and *Dancing with the Stars* and was executive producer for *Deaf U,* a reality series about Deaf and hard-of-hearing students at Gallaudet University. Of his work in Hollywood for more authentic representation of the Deaf experience, he emphasized, "We've worked for so long to create amazing content and amazing stories, and hearing people have always wanted to fix us . . . when in fact we just want to be included at the table." For Hollywood, he pointed out, more inclusion means more stories.

For the interview itself, we harnessed the power of several sight and sound technologies. Elizabeth and I communicated with Nyle with the assistance of his sign-language interpreter, and the four of us connected on a video screen. Later, the interview was posted on audio players as well as the YouTube video player, where it appeared with captions. Multiple technologies allowed people to choose to watch, listen, or read—whichever approach worked for them.

Listening Better

For people who do communicate through spoken words, making sense of speech is a complex task for our sense of hearing—aural plus oral. A widespread myth holds that in personal communication, only 7 percent of meaning is communicated through spoken words. That statistic isn't true, but it *is* true that we pay attention to far more than speech in order to understand what people are trying to communicate. We listen to the pitch of their voice, the speed and volume of the words they say, and how quickly they respond to others.

My mother told me about a new French TV show that she and my father had been watching. "It's funny," she added. "I use the subtitles, but I also want to hear the talking, even though it's in French. I adjust the volume just like I always do."

"Why, if you can't understand what they're saying?" I asked.

"Somehow, I can't make sense of what's happening if I can't hear the voices."

I tried it myself. I turned on a Danish TV show and turned off the volume—and my mother was right. The subtitles supplied the words, but without voices, it was harder to follow the action. Was this character calm, angry, or afraid? Was that character being serious or making a joke? Without hearing their voices, it was hard to know.

While our ears process speech, our eyes can also play an important role. For people with hearing loss, sight can be a vital tool for communication; for people with typical hearing levels, as much as 20 percent of comprehension comes from looking at a speaker's lips, teeth, cheeks, jaw, tongue, and head movements.

True listening is powerful. The Temple of Apollo at Delphi instructs, "Perceive what you have heard," which sounds like something Yoda would say and is easier said than done. Often, I worried about finding the right words—say, if one of my daughters brought up a problem—but I learned that I could help with not only what I *said* but how I *listened*.

For instance, studies show that when mothers listen without offering advice or criticism while their children explain solutions to problems, the children markedly improve their problem-solving ability. For adults, research has found that people speaking to attentive listeners generate better solutions than those coming up with ideas in isolation.

Often, as a listener, I suffered from convo-FOMO. In a small group, I preferred a single conversation so I didn't miss anything, and I often felt frustrated when people started side conversations. I learned, however, that this pattern is fairly inevitable: Studies of what's called the "dinner party problem" show that once a group includes five people, it usually splits into two or more conversations. So, to my relief, I gave up my attempts to try to corral many people into a single discussion.

But in my life as a listener, I faced a bigger challenge: How could

I listen better to someone who didn't want to talk? Jamie was good at listening, most of the time, but I wished he would talk more.

There are two classic strategies to get someone talking, and neither worked with Jamie. One way is to ask questions, but Jamie didn't like answering questions; another way is to get people talking about themselves, but Jamie disliked talking about himself.

He'd often deflect my attempts and keep changing the subject or goofing around until I'd find myself saying, Yogi Berra–like, "Would you please be quiet and talk?" When he did signal that he wanted to talk seriously about something, he'd often begin, and then, just as he'd started, he'd suddenly switch topics or pick up his phone.

I came up with a few strategies.

I realized that when Jamie did want to talk, I needed to listen. Often I was so pleased that he was talking that I jumped in with my own comments instead of allowing him to speak without interruptions. I also reminded myself that whenever he was ready to talk, I needed to close my book, put down my phone, or pause a TV show. If Jamie introduced some delay, like texting, I should wait quietly until he returned to our conversation.

When I started to pay more attention to our patterns, I realized that Jamie was often listening when he didn't seem to listen. Many times, I'd tell him something and he didn't appear to pay attention—but later, I'd find that he *had* listened. When I told him that I'd met someone who might be helpful to a project he was starting, he didn't say much but followed up afterward. When I mentioned a thriller that a bookish friend had loved, he didn't respond, but a few days later he bought a copy. Noticing this pattern helped me adjust my expectations: My words were heard even if they didn't always spark a response in the moment.

Listening may seem undemanding, but it's an active, taxing activity. Over the years, I've found that when I'm working on an ambitious project, I do better if I distill my thinking into concise statements. I've used my "manifesto method" to clarify my thinking with a Happiness

Manifesto, a Habits Manifesto, a Podcast Manifesto . . . and now I wrote a Manifesto for Listening. Listening to Jamie, or to anyone.

- Show my attention: Turn my body and eyes to face the other person, put down my book or phone, nod, make eye contact, say "Mmm-hmm," take notes.
- Don't rush to fill a silence.
- Ask clarifying questions; paraphrase or summarize to show that I understand—or not.
- Respect what other people want to talk about: If they raise a subject, discuss it. If they steer away from a subject, don't bring it up again unless necessary.
- Don't jump in with judgment or suggestions. (I often urge people to read a particular book.)
- Stow my phone. (One study found that the mere presence of a phone makes people sitting around a table feel more detached and less inclined to start a meaningful conversation.)
- Listen for what's *not* being said.
- Don't avoid painful subjects. (I often do this, before I'm even consciously aware of what's happening.)
- Let people talk themselves into their solution rather than supply my solution.
- When in doubt, *stop talking*.

I spent weeks tweaking my manifesto, then printed it out and stuck it on my office corkboard to keep these reminders fresh in my mind.

Not long after, I had the opportunity to put the manifesto into practice. Eleanor loves to make plans, and all through Saturday, she'd talked about how she was going to make a chocolate cake: She'd hunted down the perfect recipe, bought the ingredients, and arranged a pleasant schedule of alternating homework with completing various stages of making the cake.

On Sunday morning, in true teenager fashion, she slept very late—and Jamie went ahead and made the cake. Eleanor was outraged.

When I came home from a long walk, Eliza, who was home for spring break, rushed to tell me what I'd missed.

"I warned him!" Eliza told me. "I said, 'You'd better ask if it's okay for you to make that cake.' But he went ahead."

"Yeah, Eleanor's really mad at me," Jamie admitted. "Would you talk to her?"

"Sure," I said. "But why didn't you wait?"

"Really, I didn't think she'd care."

I found Eleanor brooding in her room. "So what happened?" I asked.

As she told her side of the story, I resisted the temptation to start crafting my responses. I just tried to listen—and not only to listen to what she was saying but also to notice the way she threw her head against the back of the chair, the way she was able to argue his side of events, the way she was talking herself into a calmer frame of mind.

I said almost nothing, but I *listened* intently, which was much harder than talking. By the end, she'd moved on from her anger. "I'll go to a thrift store," she decided. "That will be my homework break." Listening was far more helpful to Eleanor than any advice I might have given.

At that moment, Jamie stuck his head in. "I really am sorry," he repeated.

"That's okay," she said, mollified. "But next time, ask!"

"Got it." He gave a thumbs-up and turned away, obviously relieved to have been forgiven.

As I listened to this exchange, suddenly I realized that the word *listen* was just a rearrangement of the word *silent*—remarkably apt.

Making the Daily Visit

Because I was making my daily visits to the Met, I knew that, every day, I'd have time dedicated to exploring my five senses—not just what I saw, but also what I heard, smelled, touched, and even tasted. More and more, I found myself looking forward to this entry on my calendar; each time I passed through the museum's glass doors, calm descended on me. Whether I stayed for more than an hour or for just fifteen minutes, as I walked from one gallery to the next, I never knew what would catch my interest or how I might stumble across faint connections.

One aspect I loved about my visits was the Met's atmosphere of silence. No one talked to me, many rooms were quiet, and even the crowded areas had a curious quality of silence beneath the noise. I rarely heard any beeps, bangs, or shouts.

Every once in a while, I listened to music as I explored the Met's galleries. Just as a soundtrack changes the emotional tone of a movie, I could change my museum experience by listening to a song. One afternoon, I was feeling low—low energy, low mood, and low curiosity. I plodded to the Met, and, to give myself a lift, I pulled out my earbuds, chose the B-52's song "Roam," and listened to it on repeat. The music cheered me up immensely. On a different visit, I listened to Jefferson Airplane's "Today" and Cat Stevens's "Into White." Those two melancholy songs suited my contemplative mood, and I noticed that, cued by the music, I walked more slowly and looked longer at individual works.

Almost always, though, I preferred to make my visit in silence. There's a trend for museums (and churches, restaurants, and many kinds of spaces) to be more casual, loud, and relaxed, and I enjoyed the Met's formal, restrained, and meditative atmosphere. Each time I stepped from the Great Hall balcony into the gallery of monumental depictions of the Buddha, I felt relief as the echoing conversations suddenly dropped into stillness.

During my time at the Met, I often made a point to visit one of its nine fountains. The peaceful, natural murmur of water added variety to the museum's soundscapes, and the water's movement brought fresh energy to rooms where the art stood motionless.

One afternoon, after stopping to examine a pierced window screen from India, I sat down on a wooden bench in the small Moroccan Court. I admired the way this area was set off from its neighboring galleries by carved arches and columns, with an illuminated panel overhead to suggest a sunny courtyard.

In the center, framed by glazed tiles in bright, intricate patterns of green and blue, stood a fountain in a low white scalloped stone bowl. Because the water bubbled up just below its undulating surface, it made no splash—yet, faint as it was, the watery sound made the room come alive.

The sound of actual water was essential; playing a recording wouldn't have had the same effect. The burbling water was part of this time, this actual experience that could never be repeated. I hadn't clicked a link or turned a page; I'd traveled to put my body onto this bench, on this afternoon. Nothing could replace the particular experience of hearing water echoing against stone—the feeling of this moment, of *life,* in all its intensity and evanescence.

When I started this experiment, I'd expected to enjoy my daily visits to the Met, but in truth, I'd also expected to find it a bit of a burden, a task to be crossed off my daily to-do list.

But that's not how I felt. I *loved* going to the Met.

My visits were an invigorating contrast to the way I usually spent my time. I was walking, not sitting; silent in a crowd rather than alone at my desk or talking to other people; focused on my body's eye rather than my mind's eye; doing what I felt like doing rather than making the most efficient use of my time.

To help myself pay attention, I sometimes used the techniques that Sarah had suggested: holding up my hand to block off part of an artwork, squinting at it, or using a hand mirror to look at its reflection. Other days, I played "Met Roulette." I'd bought a huge book about the Met's collection, and I'd open it at random, read about an object, then go find it in the museum. Usually, though, I just wandered around.

However I spent my time at the Met, after I'd taken a break, gone for a walk, and pleased my senses, I returned to my desk with more energy. There's a relentless quality to my nature, and I get tired of all my preoccupations and ambitions. It was a relief to step out of myself and into the world.

Over the years, I'd experimented with many strategies to lower stress and deal with anxiety. Doing good deeds, talking to a friend, doing ten jumping jacks . . . I'd tried it all. The daily visit was entirely different. Instead of grappling with negative feelings, at the Met I was able to set those feelings aside.

Other people might get this refreshment from visiting a park, an inviting bookstore, or a new neighborhood. Jamie leaps at any excuse to go to the grocery store—once he went three times in a single day. For me, a museum was the right place. The peaceful self-absorption I felt made me feel connected to myself, engaged yet free.

Turning Down the Noise

At the Met and everywhere else, I loved my new appreciation of sound and silence, but my heightened awareness did have one drawback: I was more aware of unpleasant noise.

Noise might seem like a passing, inconsequential irritation, but noise pollution has terrible consequences for our health and well-being. Noise has been linked to high blood pressure, heart disease, stroke, hearing loss, anxiety, and depression. Noise makes it difficult for children to learn, interferes with sleep, raises stress levels, and promotes inflammation. Noisy hospitals make it harder for patients to sleep and heal.

Some sounds are universally disliked. One unwelcome sound—no surprise—is a crying baby, and another is the classic annoying sound of fingernails on a blackboard. Research shows that no matter what our age, sex, or culture, we *really* don't like those sounds.

Circumstances and control affect how bothersome a noise is.

When I took my laptop to a small neighborhood library to write in its quiet workroom, I got distracted by someone's cough, but when I worked in a bustling coffee shop, the conversation around me actually helped me to concentrate. The blender's noise doesn't bother me when I'm using it, but I'm annoyed when Jamie bangs around in the kitchen.

Because sudden, unexpected changes of noise can wake or distract us, many people use artificial noise to drown out the sound of barking dogs or talkative colleagues. White noise, pink noise, brown noise, and blue noise offer different "colors" of continuous signals at particular frequencies and amplitude.

I went online to compare different colors of noise. *White* encompassed all audible frequencies and reminded me of TV static; *pink* was a mix of frequencies, with reduced higher frequencies, with a sound closer to ocean waves or falling rain; *brown* sounded lower, with the hint of a rumble, like a strong wind; *blue* was higher, with a hissing quality, like water spraying from a hose; *green* supposedly captured the background sound of nature; *black* noise was . . . silence. My favorite was pink noise, and I also liked recordings of the sounds of nature—"light rain in a forest" or "babbling brook"—which, research confirms, can help us feel calmer and more relaxed. Different types of sound, I realized, could help put me into particular states of mind.

One noisy place that I wish I could make quieter? Restaurants. And I'm not alone. Consumer surveys show that "excessive noise" is a top complaint of diners, and several trends have made restaurants noisier. Instead of the muffling effects of old-fashioned touches like thick carpets, heavy curtains, tablecloths, and plush upholstery, restaurants now feature open kitchens and hard surfaces like slate, stainless steel, and wood that send noise bouncing around a room. Restaurants embrace these trends: The look is more up-to-date; it's cheaper (it's easier to clean hard surfaces, and sound-absorbing materials are expensive); and it may help boost profits, because research shows that in noisier places, people eat more quickly. However, research also suggests that loud noise can impair our ability to taste.

I'd never liked loud restaurants, yet I never tried to shape the noise environment when deciding where to eat. Big mistake!

One evening, we met some friends at a restaurant that had great food but failed the "shout test": If people have to shout for me to hear them, or if I can't understand them speaking from an arm's length, the sound is probably too loud and could eventually cause hearing loss. When we walked out the door at the evening's end, I felt relief wash over me as the noise fell away. The next time we picked a restaurant, I vowed, I'd consider the sound quality as well as the food quality.

As I became more attentive to my hearing, I found that I became more irritated by the constant drone of Muzak in stores, airports, restaurants, and even outdoor sidewalks; I hadn't chosen it, I couldn't turn it off, and I couldn't adjust the volume. In any event, that sort of background music is usually playing not to please us but to manipulate us. Just as restaurants use loud, fast music to encourage people to eat and drink faster, grocery stores pipe in slow music to encourage shoppers to linger. More time in the store means more revenue per shopper.

A friend figured out a trick for using musical noise. "In college," he told me, "to get people to clear out after a party, I'd play a loop of Air Supply singing 'I'm All Out of Love.' People rushed to leave!" Along those lines, some 7-Eleven and Rite Aid stores play music— classical, Barry Manilow—over and over to discourage people from lingering out front.

In my own life, I could shape my auditory environment both by adding sounds I liked and by eliminating sounds I didn't like. Just as I did periodic sweeps of my apartment and office to clear clutter, I needed to clear clatter.

To turn down the noise, I asked Jamie to use earbuds when he was on video calls so I didn't have to overhear garbled voices. To cut down on spam phone calls, I registered our home phone number and my cellphone number with the National Do Not Call Registry. I turned my phone to Silent Mode to minimize the distraction of my phone—the fauxcellarm or ringxiety I felt when I imagined I heard my phone ring or vibrate.

On his bedside table, Jamie kept a clock radio, and somehow he'd accidentally hit a setting that caused it to start beeping every day at noon. For months, I just turned off the alarm whenever I heard it; I finally decided to figure out how to turn the alarm off altogether. (Which took me about four seconds.) Earsore eliminated.

Speaking of the clock radio, for our whole marriage, Jamie and I had listened to all-news radio throughout the night, and it seemed likely that this constant exposure to noise might be bad for our ears. Eliza or Eleanor would walk into our bedroom and say, "It's too loud! You've got to turn that down!" So I convinced Jamie that we should change our listening habits, and now we listen to a podcast at low volume, and we use the "Sleep Timer" function so that it turns off after thirty minutes.

I was on constant alert for ways to turn down the noise. At a conference, I was impressed when the host silenced the crowd by blowing on a harmonica—he didn't even *play* the harmonica, he just blew on it. More dignified than yelling for silence, and more pleasing to the ear than banging a fork against a glass.

Small changes yield surprisingly large benefits.

Turning Up the Silence

Just as I was paying more attention to sound, I tried to notice a beautiful silence whenever I encountered it. I've always loved sounds that border on silence: wood ash dropping in a fireplace; the stately, noiseless movements of cats and swans; the whisper of hair falling when I am getting my hair cut. And I've always been deeply attracted to silence. I'm fascinated by contemplative religious orders that emphasize silence—I'm a devoted student of Saint Thérèse of Lisieux, who was a member of the Carmelite Order—and I've read many accounts by ordinary people about their quests for silence.

Each time I headed into Central Park, its busy outskirts were noisy with traffic, construction, and people. Deep inside the park, however, the city noise receded so that I could hear birdsong and the wind in the trees. This city quiet had a particularly beautiful quality, the exquisite silence that falls after a bus passes, or a car engine ticks off, or an air conditioner sighs and stops.

In my own life, I'd started to crave more silence.

For one thing, I'd started to feel talked out—as if I'd crossed some natural boundary. Over the course of a lifetime, I learned, the average person says about five hundred million words, and each day, both men and women speak about sixteen thousands words. I wondered if I'd exceeded my allotment; my words felt strained and stretched, like jam scraped too thin across a slice of toast.

A fellow writer and podcaster told me that she'd had the same experience. "It's like I have a finite number of words available to me every day," she said, "and somehow I know when I've used them all."

"Exactly!" I said.

One way to get more silence, I figured, was to go on a silent retreat, and I searched online for a place to go. I vaguely imagined staying at some sort of repurposed monastery, but when I investigated, I found that most silent retreats were focused on meditation, which I didn't want to do. I wanted silence for its own sake.

I also realized that traveling to a new place would be an *adventure* where I'd be distracted by the landscape, the lodgings, the food, and, most of all, the other people. For this exercise, I didn't want adventure; I wanted silence and, with it, solitude. And I could find silence and solitude right at home, if I planned right.

So instead of leaving my family behind to travel elsewhere, I packed them off to visit my in-laws for the weekend while I stayed behind. Many people love to go out; I love to stay home.

For three days, I didn't say a word, listen to a podcast or audiobook, watch TV, or listen to music. I live in crowded New York City, so when I went outside, I did hear music and people speaking, but no one talked to me.

I loved it. The silence refreshed me. I felt relaxed in a way that I'd never felt before.

At the same time, while I relished living in this silence, I was surprised by how often I forgot to notice it. My thoughts created their own noise. I registered the silence when I couldn't listen to a podcast as I started my daily walk, but once I began walking, I never thought about it again.

Also, I was surprised by how noisy my silence was. From outside my apartment, I heard sirens, honking trucks, revving motorcycles, barking dogs, and the thudding of music from cars as they passed; from the inside I heard the clanking of our building's elevator and the clicks, dings, and hum made by various household devices. These sounds didn't bother me, and I realized that what I sought wasn't a pure silence but rather a *human* silence. Research shows that when we're awake, we spend about a third of our time speaking or listening to others, and it was this noise that I wanted to hush.

My Silent Home Retreat helped me understand my own habits better. When I'm in an intense writing period, I often get up at 4:30 or 5:00 A.M. to work. I'd always assumed that I made this shift to take advantage of my morning-person energy patterns; in fact, I realized, I also did it to give myself hours of silence before my family and the city woke up.

I observed something paradoxical: A deep quiet had a kind of roar to it, while a few faint noises made a silence more gentle, more pleasant. A few years ago, I was fast asleep in a hotel in Tupelo, Mississippi, when the blast of a railroad whistle jerked me awake. With that sound, I was transported back to being a child, tucked into bed in my grandparents' house amid the Great Plains in North Platte, Nebraska. There, I'd often hear the railroad whistle in the middle of the night, and because my grandfather was an engineer on the Union Pacific Railroad, the sound gave me a special sense of pride and connection. It was a wild and free sound, and it also made me feel safe and protected. With that whistle and that childhood memory, the silence that returned to my hotel room felt much cozier.

I loved my silent retreat, but three days was enough. I was happy when I heard the thump of the front door and Eleanor yelling, "We're back!"

Hearing More

Before starting my experiment, I'd been enthusiastic about my foreground senses of sight and smell, but I'd neglected my hearing. Now, by pulling my sense of hearing out from the background, I'd become more aware of the pleasures of music, the mystery of conversation, the pure fun of laughter, and the restfulness of silence.

The more I listened, the more I wanted to listen. I paused to enjoy the crinkle when I popped two Pepto-Bismol tablets out of their wrapper or when—it surprised me, every time—I heard the call of a seagull as I sat at my desk. Also, my weekend alone had shown me how restorative silence could be. For me, this was another of sound's superpowers: If the banging in my head got too loud, some silence would help.

Now that I understood my song-specific way of appreciating music, I took much more pleasure in it. Instead of feeling vaguely guilty that I never made any effort to listen to new music or to expand my musical knowledge, I made careful note every time I heard a song I loved. One evening, as I was waiting for a friend to arrive at a restaurant, I heard Stevie Wonder's "Superstition" over the sound system. Instead of absent-mindedly noticing, "Oh, what a great song," I pulled out my phone and added the song to my Audio Apothecary.

Because I'd overlooked music for so long, this change gave me a surprising boost in happiness. It also gave me a new identity; instead of telling myself, "I'm not much of a music lover," I could say, "I'm a passionate song lover."

Maybe because I was listening to more music, I was experiencing more earworms, those bits of music that get stuck on repeat in the mind. Oddly, I wasn't getting earworms from music I'd heard recently, but instead from songs that I hadn't heard in a while—like the day that Prince's "Kiss" kept playing on an internal loop. Was I getting more earworms because I'd activated the music part of my brain? Or was I just paying more attention to music generally, even to the music playing in my head? I wasn't sure.

I was getting more pleasure from music and silence, but even more important was the greater connection I felt with the people around me. I was *listening* better—which made me more loving, more understanding, and more helpful. When Eleanor told me a long story about how she'd been pulled into an awkward situation among her friends, instead of interrupting with advice, I managed (mostly) to stick to comments like "Then what did you say?" or "That sounds really upsetting."

Plus I was laughing more. I'd recently discovered that I loved bouillon, and one afternoon I was praising its deliciousness to Eleanor and Jamie. "But what *is* it?" Eleanor asked suspiciously. "It's just broth," I explained—but then couldn't stop laughing. The sound of the word struck me as hilarious. "Broth, broth, broth!" I chanted. "The word has lost all meaning!" They didn't see what I found so funny, and really, neither did I, but once we started we couldn't stop laughing.

As I reflected on what I'd learned from my investigations of sight and hearing, I realized that my experiment was helping me to stay grounded in my body.

In general, I was high-strung and jumpy, and I easily got agitated and rattled. When I felt anxious, I started talking too fast, I paced, I wrung my hands like a bad actor.

By attending to my senses, I could give myself a healthy respite from my usual worries. I could slip away from bad feelings by pausing to watch as white cream slowly laced its way through black coffee, or to listen to the grinding rattle of a snowplow pushing its way down an avenue during a storm—a sound that, for some reason, I've always loved.

Unlike the distractions of the digital world, which tried to hijack my mind, this purposeful redirection of my attention to my physical surroundings gave me a boost of vitality and feeling of connection.

My body was a refuge; I could return to it again and again to calm my soul.

Smelling

The Fragrance of Hot Sun, or Why "Unscented" Is a Scent

His first consciousness was a sense of the light dry wind blowing in through the windows, with the fragrance of hot sun and sage-brush and sweet clover; a wind that made one's body feel light and one's heart cry "To-day, to-day," like a child's.

—WILLA CATHER, *Death Comes for the Archbishop*

NOT LONG AGO, I WALKED INTO AN OFFICE-BUILDING LOBBY THAT featured a water sculpture surrounded by plants—something that might have looked stylish in the 1970s. The plants looked bedraggled, the sculpture looked dated, but that didn't matter; what stopped me in my tracks wasn't how it looked but how it *smelled*.

When I was a child, every week we went to our neighborhood library. Children's books were downstairs, adult books were upstairs—and along one side of the building, behind glass, stood a two-story fountain surrounded by plants. This unconventional fountain was one narrow, transparent, sixteen-foot vertical tube in which water bubbled up, up, up until it reached the top, flowed over the lip, and ran smoothly down the sides.

The library fountain had a particular smell, a mix of water and dirt. The scent was neither bad nor good, just distinctive, and it was also remarkable as an outdoor smell brought inside. (I'm always fascinated when the inside goes outside or the outside comes inside—like an umbrella on a stage.) Eventually, the library was renovated and the fountain disappeared; I hadn't thought of it in decades. As I entered that office building, the smell of the lobby took me right back to that library.

I was overwhelmed by the memory of standing by myself, watching the water's slow progress while my mother and my baby sister waited patiently for me by the circulation desk. I felt the deep childhood pleasure of visiting the library on a cold winter day.

That smell gave me back that lost library, one of the places that I've loved most in my life. I recognized every librarian and knew every corner of its two floors, and, at the same time, its books enticed me with their promises of limitless new adventure.

I inhaled several deep breaths, and then, refreshed, walked on to the elevator.

WHILE I'D STARTED MY FIVE-SENSES investigation without much appreciation for hearing, I was already a true enthusiast for my sense of smell.

I *loved* my sense of smell. Because I couldn't experience it for long, a scent tied me to the present moment and, at the same time, it could transport me into my past—the smell of eucalyptus always reminded me of the ten months I lived in San Francisco. I could indulge in beautiful smells without spending any money, time, or energy. Also, my sense of smell helped me by being a nosy reporter. When I left my building one bright Wednesday morning, I received several neighborhood updates: Today was trash day; the food cart on our corner was frying bacon; and a passerby was enjoying some early-morning marijuana.

Those smells seemed to come to me through my nostrils, but in fact, our ability to smell arises from specialized sensory receptor cells located high inside the nose. When a pizza box flips open, microscopic molecules pass through the nostrils and stimulate those receptors, which send electrical signals to the olfactory bulb located in the brain. From there, the signal is relayed to other brain areas for identification, associations with memory and emotion, and sensory integration.

I was surprised to learn, however, that a smell can also reach those olfactory sensory neurons through the *mouth*. We smell the pizza by sniffing in through the nose, yes, but in retronasal olfaction, we also smell food when it's in our mouth; as we exhale, food scents are sent through an opening at the back of the mouth, up to the nose.

This process plays a crucial role in allowing us to experience the pleasures of food and drink. When we put something in our mouths, smell and taste combine to give us its "flavor." We need the sense of smell to experience a complex flavor, because without it, we get merely the basic tastes of sweet, salty, bitter, sour, and umami. I tested this phenomenon: I plugged my nose, put a Jelly Belly in my mouth, and got a big hit of plain *sweet,* and when I unplugged my nose, I got a complex, distinct flavor of *cherry.* (To make my sense of smell more acute, I learned, I could try increasing blood flow to my nose. Apparently, researchers and perfumers sometimes run up and down stairs to wake up their noses.)

The sense of smell, like all the senses, gives us valuable information about our environment. It alerts us to smells that we've learned to associate with danger, like fire, rotting food, and filth, as well as to enticing possibilities, like a new car and a used bookstore.

I liked the smell of nutmeg and disliked the smell of mildew, but as counterintuitive as it seems, I discovered that while we're born with innate reactions to tastes, we don't have the same kind of strong inborn responses to smell. This makes sense: When we eat something, it can hurt us, so it's important that even a newborn can reject the bitter taste that often signals poison, and favor the sweet taste that often accompanies nourishment. But nature doesn't threaten us with killer smells, and whether we think the smell of hyacinth, skunk, or spoiled milk is "good" or "bad" depends on what our mother ate before we were born, our culture, our personal history, our health conditions, and changing fashions. Because our expectations shape our experience, we respond differently to the same scent if we're in a context that tells us "Parmesan cheese" vs. "vomit," or "pine tree" vs. "disinfectant cleaner."

Does gasoline smell good or bad? People disagree. What's the smell of "fresh"—is it pine, flowers, the ocean? Claims that "citrus is cheering" and "peppermint is energizing" are based purely on learned associations. Americans find the smell of lavender "relaxing," but people from Brazil consider it "invigorating." When the Department of Defense asked cognitive psychologist Pamela Dalton to develop a stink bomb, her research showed that people often completely disagreed about what stank. A real estate broker told me, "I remind my clients, 'Clean doesn't have a smell.' You don't know how people will react, so don't scent things up. Just get rid of smells."

As with all the senses, familiarity with a smell may change our enjoyment of it. Just as I'd been bewildered by the song "'81" until I'd heard it many times, I'd always disliked Carnal Flower, a heady, sharp, overripe floral perfume, until one day when I came across a sampler for it in a department store. I gave it a sniff and suddenly loved it so much that I bought a bottle and wore it every day for weeks.

But even with my enthusiasm for Carnal Flower, I couldn't smell the fragrance as much as I wanted. The nose is a difference detector: Its job isn't to provide a consistent impression of smells but rather to signal a change that might mean possibility or danger. Therefore, in what's called "odor fatigue" or "olfactory adaptation," a smell begins to fade as soon as we've processed it.

Just one minute of deep breathing can make a smell start to recede. When I walk into a coffee shop, I enjoy the smell of coffee, but before long the smell fades. If I worked as a barista for a few months, that adjustment would happen almost as soon as I walked through the door. In fact, the stronger and more consistent the smell, the more we adapt to it. As "smell scientist" Avery Gilbert points out, "Ten minutes on the processing floor of the garlic factory will cause more adaptation than ten minutes talking to someone with garlic breath."

Because of adaptation, I can't smell my home the way a guest would smell it. I worry that our apartment smells like dog food and I just don't realize it. With sound, I can tune out some background noise, but if I turn my attention to it, I can hear it. Not so with smell—it has to become unfamiliar before it can be detected again. To know what my apartment smells like, I'd need to leave for a week.

Back in 2015, my sense of smell surprised me one night. I woke up to go to the bathroom, and as I sleepily sat up in bed, the smell of smoke jolted me into alertness. "Wake up!" I shook Jamie. "I smell fire!" I jumped to my feet and raced through the apartment, but nothing seemed amiss.

I ran back to our bedroom, where Jamie was still in bed. "Don't you smell it? What's burning?" I tend to overreact, so I was both gratified and worried when he said slowly, "Yeah, I smell it, too." Then I thought to open the window—and the smell became much stronger.

"Let's listen to the radio," Jamie said. "It seems like it's coming from outside." We didn't have to listen long before we learned that a big fire was raging in a New Jersey apartment building near the Hudson River.

If that fire had been in our building, I would've been very lucky to need that nighttime trip to the bathroom. Unlike sound, I learned, smell doesn't wake us from sleep.

Although few people are born without a sense of smell, as we age, smell loss becomes more common. Typically, in the West, people have tended to underrate the sense of smell and to consider it an insignificant sense—a sort of pleasant add-on feature—while other cultures give it greater emphasis. For instance, the Onge people of the Andaman Islands place far more importance on smell: Their calendar is designed around the fragrances of the plants that bloom at particular times, and they greet each other by inquiring, "How is your nose?"

In the United States and elsewhere, the Covid-19 pandemic changed the tendency to undervalue the sense of smell. Because infection can cause loss or alteration of the sense of smell—and with it, taste—people realized smell's importance.

After she got Covid-19, a friend lost her senses of smell and taste for a few months. She told me, "I felt claustrophobic, the world felt stale and airless. I drank a lot of kombucha because the vinegar and fizz combo gave me some sensation. I had to add walnuts and dried fruit to my oatmeal, for texture."

Whatever the cause, people who can't smell miss important warnings, such as the smell of meat that's gone bad, smoke, and leaking gas. They have trouble eating healthfully: Some people lose weight because food no longer tastes good, while others gain weight because food never seems satisfying.

Without smells, people report feeling cut off from their surroundings. I briefly suffered this disconnection when I had a bad cold. Because I couldn't smell the carriage horses as they waited to take passengers on a ride, or the watery smell of the boat pond, my walk in Central Park felt flat and unreal; I felt as if I were watching a movie or trapped behind a pane of glass.

Worst of all, the loss of smell can make people feel isolated. One woman emailed me: "When I lost my sense of smell from Covid, the smell I missed most was the smell of my husband when I rested my head on his chest at night."

Compared to the other senses, smell seems the most crude. There's something animalistic and unrefined about smelling or even talking about a smell, especially a bodily smell. The tradition of the executive bathroom has always astonished me with its frank acknowledgment of this aspect of human society.

Usually it seems rude to be caught smelling something in public—even food. Once, while going through a buffet line, I encountered a giant cauldron of soup. I didn't know if I'd like "Seafood Cioppino" or not, so I leaned forward and took a deep sniff. Even as I was doing it, I was thinking, "This is a major violation of social norms," and sure enough, the woman standing next to me said, "Come on! What are you doing?" I apologized and rushed off, but really, what was the harm? My face was nowhere near the soup, yet it felt wrong to be sniffing that way. Perhaps only flowers or a perfume counter allow us to smell deeply with good manners.

Educating My Nose

Because I appreciated it so much, I wanted to do more to explore and enjoy my sense of smell. I loved the holiday scent of paper-white narcissus flowers, but each December I told myself, "Why spend the money and the hassle to get them? I'll get flowers next year." And I never did. Now I resolved to buy those flowers.

Too often, I allowed sensations to fade into the background and barely registered the information my nose was providing. And while I valued my sense of smell, I didn't know much about it. When we love something, we want to study it; the more we bring to an experience, the more we get from it. While many people study music, art, movies, food, and wine to appreciate them better, few people try to educate their sense of smell. I decided to take a class.

One advantage of living in New York City was that I could find a course on just about any subject. The Pratt Institute offered two six-week courses, "Introduction to Perfumery Technique and the Language of Scent" and "Advanced Perfumery," and I signed up for both.

That first Saturday morning, I took the subway down to Fourteenth Street and Seventh Avenue, where Brooklyn-based Pratt has its satellite building. Because I love any chance to walk around work-places or schools, to spy on how other people spend their days and organize their spaces, I arrived early. I read the notices on the bulletin board, I looked at the snacks stocked in the vending machines, I peered into the professors' offices. Finally I headed to my classroom.

We took our seats on uncomfortable high stools set around lab tables, which reinforced the science-class nature of the course. My fellow students were mostly in their twenties, thirties, or forties, with a mix of backgrounds, outgoingness, and coolness. We went around the room to introduce ourselves, and I learned that many of them wanted to become perfumers, while others worked in completely different fields, like refugee advocacy, and wanted to explore a subject that was completely outside their usual concerns. Given that I wrote so much about happiness, it seemed auspicious that our professor, Raymond Matts, was the scent designer of the Clinique blockbuster fragrance Happy.

Over the following weeks, we worked through the history of perfume, the mechanics of the sense of smell, the descriptive language of fragrance, and the composition of a perfume.

In every class, our professor was full of advice, admonitions, and pronouncements, and I filled my notebook with his instruction.

"Don't use coffee beans to clear your nose, that's a myth. Instead, smell the crook of your elbow. That's your own smell."

"Don't layer. Fine fragrances are complex, and created with careful balance."

"Don't judge a fragrance by smelling the atomizer of a bottle. Test it on your skin."

"Don't confuse 'fruity' and 'citrus.' They're totally different."

"Don't spray fragrance into the air and walk through it."

"To make a beautiful fragrance, it's often necessary to add some bad-smelling notes."

"Some people say they don't want 'chemicals' in their fragrance, but everything is a chemical. *Water* is a chemical."

"Smell everything. Snap a twig, sniff the inside of a leather bag, scrape an orange, smell your stinky feet."

"To use a blotter properly, hold it at one end, spray or dip the tip, wait for it to dry, then move the strip back and forth under both nostrils. Each nostril senses slightly differently."

I'd never realized that just as having two eyes gives us depth perception, and having two ears helps us pinpoint the origin of sounds, having two nostrils gives us more sophisticated smell perception. The nostrils differ slightly in how fast they suck in air, and this difference allows each nostril to deliver slightly different information to the brain. When I got home, I pulled out a jar of capers and smelled first with my left nostril, then with my right. The smell did indeed change when I switched from side to side, and I got a richer hit when I sniffed with both nostrils together.

In the class, we learned that fragrances are made of "notes," or scents perceived, that are sorted into three categories according to how quickly the note appears once the fragrance is applied. The different categories of notes form an olfactory pyramid, in which top notes are perceived immediately, middle notes emerge as the top notes dissipate, and base notes emerge later and help to sustain the other notes. Together, these notes create the fragrance experience.

In the Advanced Perfumery classes, we sniffed our way from top to bottom through the eighteen categories of the olfactory pyramid. We started with the top notes, with Citrus at the pyramid's peak, along with notes such as New Freshness and Aromatic, then continued through middle notes such as Green and Aldehyde, and concluded with base notes such as Amber, Powdery, and at the very bottom, Musk. My (utterly unoriginal) favorite category was Floral.

It was challenging to dip a blotter into a vial of clear liquid, pull it out, smell it, and try to put the experience into words. My classmates and I would say things like, "This reminds me of cut grass drying in the sun," "This smells like dishwashing soap," "This makes me think of a hot cedar closet," or canned corn, wet toilet paper, cooked carrots, or a swimming pool.

One Saturday after another, we perched on our stools and smelled. During our study of base notes, I discovered that I liked Myrrh and didn't like Labdanum, but when we reached the pyramid's final category of Musk, I was puzzled. As usual, we were dipping our blotters into the vials and taking deep whiffs, but I wasn't getting any impressions. Was this an emperor's-new-clothes situation? Everyone else was carrying on as usual.

"Can you smell anything?" I asked my neighbor in a low voice.

"Sure," he said with surprise. "Don't you?"

"Not really."

"Maybe your strips didn't get dipped. Try mine." He handed me his blotter strips, but still—nothing.

I felt sheepish when I raised my hand to say, "I don't think I smell anything."

"Maybe not," said my professor matter-of-factly. "A fair number of people can't smell Musk."

Initially, I was relieved—but wait, I was missing a smell? Musk, we'd learned, had been very popular since the 1990s; it's easy to combine with other scents and rounds out a fragrance—plus it's inexpensive to manufacture. I felt left out as my classmates took deep, thoughtful sniffs and wrote notes on ambrettolide or ethylene brassylate. I'd never realized that I wasn't able to experience a category of smell.

By the time we smelled our way through the entire olfactory pyramid, I had an even deeper appreciation of the power of my nose. Before the course, I wouldn't have predicted how much I would love unpoetically named scents such as methyl ionone gamma, which reminded me of fancy European fruit-flavored hard candies; stemone, which recalled the sharp, green, crushed-leaf smell of a florist's shop; and perhaps my favorite, the gorgeous phenylethyl alcohol, with its dawn rose-petal freshness.

My study of scent inspired me to wear perfume more frequently.

These days, because many people prefer a perfume-free environment, I wouldn't wear it to a meeting or a restaurant—but usually I worked at home, so why not put it on? I also started to wear perfume each night. It felt so luxurious.

I splurged and bought myself a perfume sampler. I love all things systematic and taxonomic: an artist's palette, a plastic pill organizer, a tackle box, the Linnaean taxonomy, an Advent calendar, the periodic table of the elements. I loved spraying my way through an orderly row of cunning little bottles.

Before I'd started my five-senses experiment, I'd considered my sense of smell one of my foreground senses, but looking back, I hadn't been as attuned to smell as I'd thought. This class had trained me to pay much closer attention.

Also, I decided that if I ever started a fragrance business, I'd call it the Ol' Factory, of scents to be sensed.

What's That Smell?

Throughout my fragrance classes, my professor repeatedly reminded us to stay alert to all the smells that surround us.

When I asked on social media, "Do you pay much attention to your sense of smell?" the answers showed that some people are far more attuned to smell than others. Some take a professional interest, such as the flavor-industry expert who responded, "I'm a professional smeller, 'un nez.' I'm the one who knows immediately if someone has changed their perfume." A microbiologist explained how the scientists in her clinical hospital lab use their sense of smell:

> Often we can tell what organism we have in a culture by its smell. Some smell like grapes, butterscotch, chocolate cake, fruit, bleach, dirt, and many with unique smells all their own. Some of us can smell specific organisms better than others can, and some people can't smell certain ones at all.

Other people are smell amateurs who are just good at paying attention, like the friend who told me, "I know when my teenage son has been drinking with his friends, and he can't figure out how I do it! He must have heard that peanut butter covers up the smell of alcohol. Now I know that whenever he smells like peanut butter, he's been up to mischief."

As part of my efforts to cultivate my sense of smell, I tried to do a better job of putting accurate names to smells. Was that soap orange-scented or grapefruit-scented? What spice could I smell in the kitchen—rosemary or thyme? It was a fun challenge.

In just about every discussion of smell, I'd read about the "tip-of-the-nose phenomenon": If we're presented with familiar smells but can't see what they're coming from, we often have trouble identifying them; our brains struggle to retrieve the verbal information linked to the smell. (When we're given a selection of possible labels from which to choose, we do better.) Research suggests that people of different cultures perform better or worse at this task; for instance, the Jahai people of Malaysia have more sophisticated terms to describe smells and are more accurate in naming what they smell than people from many other cultures.

"Let's play a game," I suggested to Eliza and Eleanor one afternoon. "We'll test each other's sense of smell, and we'll see who scores the highest."

"Do we have to smell anything bad?" asked Eleanor.

"No, just ordinary things from around the apartment," I said.

We took turns getting blindfolded and sniffing mystery scents such as mustard, lime juice, and coffee. Contrary to the difficulty we were supposed to face, we all named most of the smells easily. I was stumped by vinegar, Eliza mislabeled cloves as nutmeg, and Eleanor guessed butterscotch for caramel sauce.

This task wasn't as difficult as I'd been led to expect.

However, a few weeks later, I bought Follow Your Nose, a bingo-like board game where players compete to identify familiar scents.

The box held thirty small, white plastic containers with lids that popped off to release different aromas, such as hazelnut, soap, and grass. To win, players matched the smell containers to their identifying pictures. Eliza, Eleanor, and I took a few turns, then stopped playing the game and just worked together to try to identify the smells. We were surprised by how difficult it was.

"I know I recognize this smell," Eliza said, holding up a container, "but I can't quite place it." She passed it to me. "Why was identifying smells so much easier when we did it before, with the real smells from the apartment?"

"I have no idea," I said after giving the container a sniff. "This is much harder—but why?"

It was an odd feeling. I'd smell a very familiar scent but not have any idea how to categorize it, and then, after I'd reviewed the thirty options and decided I was smelling "chimney" or "rose," the scent would instantly become unmistakable. Once I had a word for what I was experiencing, my brain and senses clicked together.

The pleasure of Follow Your Nose reminded me of scratch-and-sniff, one of my favorite ways to have fun with smell. I've always been fascinated by scratch-and-sniffs—the closest thing we can get to a photo of a scent.

As a child, my sister Elizabeth collected scratch-and-sniff stickers, and recently, when I visited my parents, I hunted down the wicker basket that still holds her collection and sniffed away at my favorites. Even all these years later, they still deliver a delightful hit of grape, pickle, and popcorn.

Finding those old stickers made me curious about the contemporary choices of scratch-and-sniff, and I couldn't resist buying myself a pack. I still got a kick from scratching and smelling cherry pie, birthday cake, banana. The next time I left a list of tasks for Eleanor to do, I added a blueberry scratch-and-sniff sticker to my instructions.

Playing with these smells reminded me that I'd always been curious about smelling salts. While I associated smelling salts with crystal vials and delicate Victorian ladies, I learned that these days, they were called "ammonia inhalants" and marketed to athletes. I ordered a box.

Smelling salts work because the ammonia gas irritates the mucous membranes of the nose and lungs, triggering an inhalation reflex—which sounded a bit scary. It took me a few days to work up the nerve to pop one of the capsules, but I finally squeezed one between my fingers and took a whiff. It wasn't a terrible smell, but it was an *uncanny* smell—it didn't feel like a smell, it felt like chlorinated water going up my nose. I couldn't help but jerk my head back.

Curiosity satisfied.

Adding Fragrance and Eliminating Odor

One way to gain happiness is to get more of what makes us feel *good* (like a pineapple scratch-and-sniff); another way is to eliminate what makes us feel *bad*.

In the past, I realized, I'd been far too passive about accepting sensory experiences. I hadn't thought much about how I could get more joy from my surroundings—whether by boosting delight or eliminating nastiness. I decided to look for ways to add good smells to my life, and also eliminate bad smells.

First, and more fun: Add good smells.

Research shows that when we enjoy a scent, or have good memories associated with it, that smell can help put us in a happy mood. On a trip to France, I saw huge fields of lavender baking in the sun; ever since, I've loved the smell of lavender. Now I made it a habit, whenever I saw lavender growing anywhere, to pinch a sprig between my fingers and breathe in that dusty, sweet smell. At some friends' apartment, I noticed the beautiful scent of their soap, and when our soap ran out, instead of just replacing it with the same standard plain soap, I splurged to buy that nicer-smelling brand. Because I have a tendency to "save" my nicest things, I pushed myself actually to light my favorite gardenia-scented candle when I sat at my desk (but not every day, or I might get so accustomed to it that I'd lose the ability to smell it).

Also, I decided to assign one of my favorite scents to be my lucky scent. It was the Hay *accord,* or combination of fragrance ingredients, that I'd bought years ago from the unconventional scent company CB I Hate Perfume. I loved Hay's heavy, honey smell of hay, which I associated with open fields and cloudless skies, and I made a point to save Hay for times when I needed good luck.

While wearing a scent might seem completely unrelated to handling a difficult meeting, research shows that people who believe they have luck on their side feel greater self-efficacy, and this belief actually does boost performance. For instance, golfers told that a particular golf ball "has turned out to be a lucky ball" did better putting than people who weren't given that reassurance. The scent of hay allowed me to give myself a shot of encouragement.

Plus I'd discovered another helpful pattern: When one of my senses was particularly satisfied, I felt less desire to stimulate the other senses. When I felt like snacking out of boredom, if I put on perfume or did something else to gratify one of my senses, my impulse to snack faded away.

Along with adding good smells, I wanted to eliminate bad smells; getting rid of disagreeable sensations made my life happier.

We keep an open box of baking soda in our refrigerator to absorb bad smells, and when I opened the fridge door, the smell told me it was time to swap in a fresh box. As I threw away the old box, it occurred to me that while our brand of kitchen trash bags was scented with a "fresh clean" smell, in fact, I disliked that scent intensely. So, after years of putting up with it, I switched to "unscented"—though of course, "unscented" is a scent. (Just as noise-cancellation works by adding more noise, often, when a product has no scent, it's because *more scent* has been added to mask the natural smell of its ingredients.)

Also, I noticed that in addition to Barnaby's usual doggy smell, he had a new smell that seemed somehow familiar.

"Eleanor, have you noticed a different smell around Barnaby?" I asked.

"Yeah," she said. "What is it?"

"I know this sounds weird, but to me it smells like . . . corn chips," I said. "But there's no way he could be eating corn chips."

My impression of this smell seemed so idiosyncratic and incongruous that it hadn't occurred to me to look it up, but Eleanor pulled out her phone and searched.

"I found an article called 'My Dog's Paws Smell Like Fritos—Is This Normal?'" she reported two seconds later.

"This isn't just my imagination!" I felt so gratified. "So, *is* it normal?"

She scanned the article. "Yeah, it's harmless. It's from bacteria on their paws. We can just shampoo him."

Without a microscope, without a science degree, and just in passing, my mighty nose had managed to detect the presence of something far too small for me to see. We gave Barnaby a bath, and the smell disappeared.

Capturing Scent Memories

Our five senses give us information about the present state of the world—such as the state of a dog's paws—and our senses also help us to recall memories. We glimpse a long-vanished room in a photo, we hear the snatch of an old song on the radio, we bite into a food we haven't eaten since childhood, we feel the weight of an old pair of boots—and memories come flooding back.

But for many people, the sense of smell seems to hold a special power to evoke the past—perhaps for some reason related to brain wiring, or perhaps because the memories sparked by smell often overtake us without warning so we're struck by them more intensely.

We're just walking down the street or stepping into someone's house when, with a simple smell, memories return.

Recently, the city repaved the streets near my apartment, and my neighborhood smelled exactly like the asphalt plant where I worked during high school. That smell brought back memories of the constant roar of the trucks, the beeps of the machinery, and the feeling of dread that I'd make a mistake—memories that I'd forgotten.

Andy Warhol exploited the power of smell to evoke memories. He'd wear a perfume for three months and then never wear it again, so that its scent reminded him of that time. "Seeing, hearing, touching, tasting are just not as powerful as smelling if you want your whole being to go back for a second to something," he explained. "By having smells stopped up in bottles, I . . . get the memories I'm in the mood to have."

Inspired by Warhol, I bought a bottle of Tea Rose perfume. Although I've always loved this fragrance, I stopped wearing it long ago because it's unusually heavy and rich. But when I realized how vividly it reminds me of my senior year of college, when I wore it as my special party perfume, I decided to keep a bottle on a shelf as an easy way to evoke memories of that time.

Making the Daily Visit

My daily visits to the Met continued, of course, and I wanted to use each of my five senses to enrich my experience there—so I took my study of smell to the museum. Did the Met *have* a smell? Yes, many smells.

The entrance had the smell of the outdoors, the hand soap in the restrooms had a remarkably pleasant scent, and the smell of one little-used stairwell reminded me of law school. Every week, a team decorated the Great Hall with spectacular new twelve-foot flower arrangements in five stone vases, and whenever I walked past them, I tried to catch the smell of leaves and blossoms. The wood or stone materials of different galleries affected their scent—or did they? Maybe not. To a surprising extent, we experience what we expect to experience, and maybe my sense of sight was telling me what to smell.

One of my favorite galleries had smells that came as a shock. On the second floor, tucked inside a maze of galleries, the splendid Chinese Garden Court was a real garden, with the surprising scents of dirt, plants, and the water of the tiny pond where spotted koi fish swam in slow circles. These scents were fainter than I would have expected; perhaps the Met's ventilation and filtration system drew them away.

During one day's visit, as I stood in the American Wing with my back to Edward Kemeys's *Panther and Cubs* and looked at it in a hand mirror, I noticed the smell of food drifting out from the café. While I liked the restaurant's life and bustle, for me, the food smells detracted from the museum atmosphere I loved. The artworks seemed less important because they felt pushed to the outskirts of other activities.

On another visit, as I gazed at several incense burners in the gallery of art from Iran and Central Asia, I thought, "It would be so great to smell incense as I walked through this room." The museum used sunlight and the sound of water to enliven its spaces; what if it also used smells? I would love that! (A moment later, I realized that some people would hate that. Or maybe a fire feature? I could imagine the objections to that, too.)

As I walked from one gallery to the next, my sense of smell heightened my feeling of *being present*. I could experience a particular scent only right here, right now. On each visit, the museum's smells varied, just a little, from the day before. I might smell a visitor's coconut sunscreen, or a wet coat on a rainy day, or the fusty smell that always lingered near the Musical Instruments gallery.

These invisible differences illustrated the importance of the dailiness of my visits. In the past, when I'd visited the Met, I'd always had a particular goal. "I want to see *this*," I'd remind myself, "so I can't get distracted by *that*." This attitude helped me stick to my priorities but also made it harder for me to cultivate the open, searching mindset that invigorated me.

Once I started to visit the Met every day, I didn't need to use my time wisely, and I could explore every room. To my surprise, the visible-storage facility in the American Wing became one of my favorite places to wander around. Slotted into a dim mezzanine level, it held items that weren't quite worthy of the main galleries, but were still carefully preserved and organized in the Met's version of a walk-in closet. As I drifted up and down the crowded aisles, objects that I would've otherwise found boring—wooden chairs, vases of iridescent glass, silver spoons—became interesting. And I had time to look at every pitcher and picture, and to notice how the air smelled different in these tightly packed rows than it did in the Met's big, open galleries.

Writer Henry David Thoreau noted, "I love a broad margin to my life." Some people argue that we should "do nothing" or embrace "wasting time," but of course, we do *something* with time, one way or another. I'm always doing something, and yet I know that to feed my imagination, I also need to do a lot of *anything*—anything I feel drawn to do, in the moment, in a spirit of play. Looking, listening, and smelling as I walked through the galleries helped me stay in a loose, associative frame of mind. Research shows that when our attention is unfocused, we're more able to make the unexpected associations and interpretations that spark insights and solutions.

Every day in the Met, I looked for something interesting or amusing. I visited my beloved toothy cow. I searched for objects tied to books I was reading (after I read Marguerite Yourcenar's *Memoirs of Hadrian,* I looked for representations of Antinous). I made a game of looking for representations of swans, frogs, skulls. I took a special interest in any object that held supernatural power, such as a magic wand, amulet, *boli,* saint's relic, *kafigeledjo,* or written spell. I looked for objects that surprised me, because I could be surprised only if I was paying close attention: I was surprised that the museum had a potato masher and safety pins on display, and by how often the Buddha is depicted with a mustache.

One day, as I walked through a gallery, I was enjoying the familiar fragrance of a visitor's cologne—I think it was Dior's Sauvage—when suddenly I jumped back in surprise, because I'd felt the shock of a gaze. Ancient bronze eyes seemed to pop out and size me up as I walked past. Though more beautiful, a set of jasper lips didn't have the same eerie effect.

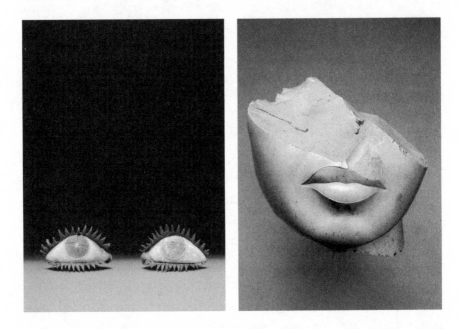

Even isolated from a face, oversize, and on a shelf, those eyes felt full of life. Now, each time I smell that cologne, I'm reminded of those eyes.

Feeling Closer to Others Through Smell

At the Met or anywhere else, the sense of smell is often easy to ignore, but it's a powerful way to engage with the world—and with other people.

It's embarrassing to talk about the desire to smell another person. There's something so intimate about breathing in the scent of someone's hair or picking up someone's T-shirt from the floor and taking a deep whiff. Yet catching that scent creates a deep sense of attachment.

Other animals and insects release *pheromones,* chemical compounds that act as a silent, invisible, powerful way to communicate information and induce a particular behavior. For instance, pheromones help animals to find mates, prompt suckling by newborns, and mediate colony activities among insects such as ants and bees.

Although an unlikely mix of scientists, sellers of perfumes and love potions, and military agencies have searched for human sex pheromones, no direct evidence has been found. While it seems possible that humans, like other animals, communicate through pheromones, researchers haven't yet been able to identify a single one.

But whether or not humans use pheromones the way other creatures do, we're deeply influenced by others' scents. A friend told me, "One night, early in our relationship, I woke up and smelled my future husband while he was sleeping to be sure I liked his smell."

"You weren't sure?"

"I was scared I wasn't going to! I was so relieved when I liked his scent."

Given our general interest in information about other people, it's perhaps surprising—or very unsurprising—that we work so hard to disguise our natural smells. To smell better to other people, we use deodorants, perfumes, showers, mouthwash, and mints to create what has been called our "diplomatic" odor. I myself own countless smell-influencing products, but until recently, I'd never heard about the "internal deodorant" Devrom—an over-the-counter, FDA-approved medication that "eliminates odor from flatulence and stool." (I didn't run out and buy any Devrom myself, but it was nice to know that it existed.)

The intimate—even almost *illicit*—aspect of the sense of smell means that we get a tremendous charge from it. It's a pleasure that feels forbidden, bold. It's embarrassing to admit, but one reason that I love the perfume Jannat is that it has a distinct note of . . . sweaty body.

Sometimes, we might not even be aware of scent's powerful influence. At a conference, I met a guy and liked him instantly—then realized that I was probably swayed by the fact that he smelled faintly of the Neutrogena shampoo that I associated with Jamie.

In the early days of moving in to our apartment, I remember how unsettled I felt by all its strange smells. The back hallway, the dishwasher, the bedroom—they didn't smell bad, exactly, but they didn't smell like *us*, which is how home is supposed to smell. Now, though, I experience the opposite effect: Those smells are so familiar that I don't even notice them. But when I come home from a trip, the smells of home welcome me back to a place of safety and love.

These days, when I make the bed in the morning, instead of just throwing everything into place, I take a moment to hold Jamie's pillow to my nose, to breathe in deeply, to appreciate the scent I love so much.

Smelling More

When I walked into the middle of Central Park, into the wild, clean, careless abundance of a late morning in spring, I thought, "I love the silence of the park." Then I actually listened and realized that the park wasn't silent at all. Sure, it was more silent than the streets that surrounded it, but I heard dogs barking, birds chirping, a distant horn honking, a child's piping voice singing, and I was able to eavesdrop on a man who was talking into the air with great animation. The park's "silence" was full of sounds, sights—and also smells.

For years, I'd been walking in the park. I usually took the same route, so that path was very familiar. But when I started paying close attention to smells, I was surprised to notice that day after day, one fifty-foot stretch had a distinctive, pleasant scent that seemed very out of place. Finally, just as I'd done in my perfume class, I stopped, focused on my nose, and tried to put words to the sensation. The smell was . . . spicy, warm, it reminded me of cider . . . cloves! I looked for some plant or food stand to explain this unexpected smell, but nothing stood out. I assumed I was the only one to detect it, until I thought to check the internet—and mystery solved. I was smelling the park's organic clove-oil weed killer.

In the park and everywhere else, with my new attention, I experienced smells more intensely. As I walked by a hair salon, a customer pushed open the door, and I gave a deep sniff as the sharp smell of hair products wafted over me. At a friend's house, I helped her son pry the lid off a new can of Play-Doh and smelled that salty, floury scent. I was even relishing disagreeable smells, like the aroma floating above our kitchen garbage pail and the scent of a subway station after heavy rain: They gave depth to sensation.

My sense of smell had the superpower of making me feel present in my body, at the present moment. Evanescence is a distinctive quality of a scent. We can't smell it over and over; we can't bookmark it, rewind it, stockpile it, or save it for later. Explicitly training my attention on the smell of a shoe store or the lobby of my daughter's school gave me a sense of being present, *of being exactly where I was, right then.* When I was going somewhere, I wanted to take my body there with me.

I was also more aware of how scent could evoke the past, and I paid attention to any memories that floated up. On a neighborhood walk, I passed a construction shed—and the woody, slightly dank smell conjured up scenes of summer camp and the fun I'd had in those flimsy, overstuffed cabins.

From my investigations into the five senses so far, some distinctions were becoming more obvious—about myself, and other people. For example, I'd noticed that some people enjoyed fewer sensory experiences, while others found much to enjoy; some had rigorous standards, while others' standards were more relaxed.

For instance, a restaurant critic is more demanding than the average diner and also has a profound appreciation for a truly exceptional meal; a foodie may also have high standards but can enjoy an excellent hot dog as much as foie gras. Elizabeth enthusiastically ate just about any food put on her plate, but she lacked discernment. When I started this project, like Elizabeth, I didn't have sophisticated standards, but unlike Elizabeth, I didn't enjoy much. With my five-senses exploration, I'd wanted both to *notice more* and to *enjoy more*. And so far, I'd made real progress.

When I started paying more attention to music, I suddenly realized how much I loved Christmas carols. I'd assumed that with my uneducated palate, all tequila tasted the same, but after Jamie and I took a tasting class during a vacation, I could distinguish among the five types—and I preferred *reposado*. Now that I knew myself better, I could go out of my way to play Christmas music and drink my favorite kind of tequila.

One afternoon, as I was walking in our neighborhood, I reached out with my sense of smell to experience this time, this place. I passed through the cool, fishy smell wafting up from a grocer's cellar door and the sweet smell that hung around the fruit stand next to it, and I breathed in the creamy scent of the gardenia tree set outside a florist shop. I loved getting a hit of nature—fish, fruit, flower—as I walked down a crowded city sidewalk to my apartment.

And I loved every familiar smell of home.

Tasting

The Taste of the Tea and the Cake, or Why Ketchup Is Magic

Whence could it have come to me, this all-powerful joy? I was conscious that it was connected with the taste of the tea and the cake, but that it infinitely transcended those savours.

—Marcel Proust, *Swann's Way*

Because it was the height of summer, the air had a baked, trapped quality. Except when I could find some shade from a building, the sun beat down on me from above and heat radiated upward from the sidewalks and streets. The breeze created by passing traffic lifted dust and trash without creating any cool relief. The sky was so bright that if I had forgotten my sunglasses, I would have had to turn back.

I was walking from a meeting to my subway stop when suddenly I felt extremely thirsty. I didn't have to walk far before I found a handy corner store, and I stepped inside to survey the contents of the beverage cooler. Alongside the usual assortment of soft drinks and energy drinks, I spotted a Snapple Diet Peach Tea. I hadn't seen that label in years. I paid and, as soon as I was back on the sidewalk, gulped down a mouthful.

The sweet, smooth, fruity flavor instantly transported me back to law school. Students were required to spend a certain amount of money in the law-school cafeteria, and I drank gallons of Diet Peach Snapple there. By the time I graduated, I was thoroughly tired of it.

But now, after so many years, the tea delighted me. After the first swig, I slowed down to savor it like an expert: I swished it around in my mouth to appreciate its over-the-top peach kick and its surprising dusty note. Its flavor brought back the intense, cloistered atmosphere of that time.

Jamie had been in law school with me, so, with difficulty, I stopped myself from finishing the whole bottle. I took it home so he could share the taste and the memory.

TASTE IS A SENSE THAT'S enormously popular, and throughout history people have gone to great lengths to pursue the delicious; the demand for flavorful ingredients such as pepper, cloves, and cinnamon altered the shape and fortunes of empires. People love taste-related activities such as cooking, exploring farmers' markets, trying new restaurants, sampling wines, and even talking, reading, and watching TV shows about taste experiences.

What we eat, with whom we eat, how we eat, and when we eat are essential choices that tie us to our identity, our memories, and our culture.

While our five senses can give us a quick lift or a pleasant distraction, we also sometimes succumb to temptations from the senses—and, in particular, to taste—in ways that aren't healthy. Few people seem bothered by their love of rap or abstract expressionism, but many people complain that they can't resist a doughnut.

For my part, I'd never been adventurous in exploring tastes. I enjoyed many foods—I just wasn't as interested in expanding my taste horizons as most other people seemed to be.

As humans, we love pattern and predictability, and we love novelty and surprise—but people differ in how much predictability or surprise they want. I eat the same foods, prepared the same way, just about every day. "New York City is wasted on you," a friend scolded me. "You could try any kind of food, but you just want to eat plain grilled salmon." Yup.

Because love of food is often held up as a marker of an enthusiasm for life, my lack of passion has always made me feel a bit inadequate. Cooking icon Julia Child declared, "People who love to eat are always the best people"; food essayist Jean Anthelme Brillat-Savarin wrote, "Tell me what you eat, and I shall tell you what you are." What did that say about *me*?

My most important personal commandment is "Be Gretchen": I wanted to accept myself and also expect more from myself. The sense of taste gives so much happiness to so many people, I couldn't help but feel that I was missing out—and that I could learn to appreciate taste more.

Much of our response to tastes, I learned, is hardwired from birth, because taste conveys the lifesaving information of whether a food is likely to be poisonous or nutritious. But how many basic taste categories can we perceive? Four, five, six, fourteen? I was surprised to learn that the number was still under debate. Because tastes such as *fatty, soapy, metallic,* and *starchy* hadn't yet been widely accepted, I decided to explore the five tastes considered standard in the West: *sweet, sour, bitter, salty,* and *umami*.

Because sweet foods often provide energy and nutrients, we're born craving sweetness, we seek it constantly, and in the last five hundred years, it has overmastered the world.

We also love salty; if we don't eat enough salt, we die. It's the only rock we eat. It's a universal flavor enhancer that lifts sweetness, deepens umami, and masks bitterness (which is why people salt their grapefruit or coffee). We tend to add more, more, more salt, until we reach the intolerable tipping point of *too salty*.

A bitter taste often signals the presence of poison, so we find it distasteful—until we learn to embrace the taste of coffee or escarole.

A sour taste signals the presence of acid in items such as limes, cranberries, yogurt, wine, and vinegar. The mouth-puckering sting of sour gives a zest to food that tastes flat, though at some point (and people differ as to what point) people find a taste too sour.

Umami, or "savory," entered the taste lineup surprisingly recently. In 1908, chemist Kikunae Ikeda proposed its existence to describe the full-bodied, meaty quality found in items such as broths, cooked meats, tomato products, walnuts, fish sauce, soy sauce, aged Parmesan cheese, and red wine. Adding the seasoning monosodium glutamate, or MSG, boosts umami (and, contrary to rumor, doesn't cause any negative health effects).

We often confuse bitter and sour, perhaps because they often appear together. I used an orange to remind myself of the difference: Biting into a segment gave me a sour taste, while chewing a piece of rind gave me a bitter taste.

The right combinations can make food and drink more delicious. The salt in Parmesan cheese helps bring out the flavors in a salad. The umami of mushrooms improves a bland sauce. The sugar in tonic water cuts the beverage's bitterness; surprisingly, a can of Schweppes tonic water contains almost as much sugar as a can of Coca-Cola, but because of quinine's bitterness, it doesn't taste nearly as sweet. I hadn't tried tonic in years, so I opened a small bottle and took a thoughtful sip. It was sweet and bitter, by turns, with a fizz of carbonation.

When it comes to taste—and the senses generally—we may dislike an item if it violates the sensory patterns we expect. Who wants Watermelon Oreos, Cheetos Lip Balm, Frito-Lay Lemonade, Touch of Yogurt Shampoo, or frozen meals from Colgate? But as improbable as it seems, these are all actual products. (Weird mash-ups do make for a good prank, however—no one expects to find ham-flavored candy canes in a Christmas stocking.)

As I'd learned in my investigation of the sense of smell, simple *taste* is quite different from more complex *flavor,* which combines taste and smell. We can taste sweet, but for the specific experience of chocolate, strawberry, or caramel, we need our sense of smell. In what's called the "olfactory location illusion" or "oral referral," we experience the food's flavor as coming through our mouth, even though our nose furnishes much of that flavor.

Genetic factors mean that some people can detect certain aspects of food—such as bitterness, sweetness, and creaminess—more intensely than others. For instance, during my fragrance class, we tested ourselves by putting phenylthiocarbamide test strips on our tongues. To me, the paper tasted slightly bitter, which marked me as a "taster," while a few "super-taster" classmates found the strips intensely bitter.

Age is a factor in how we taste, too. As we age, we may lose some of our sense of taste, often because our sense of smell isn't as acute. Children love sweets, and this love isn't just cultural; children are hardwired to prefer more intense sweetness and saltiness than adults, and they also seem more sensitive to bitterness. And, for reasons that aren't clear, children love sourness. Candy aisles are packed with popular super-sour choices—Warheads, Toxic Waste Sour Candy, Tear Jerkers—and research suggests that from about age five to nine years, kids really do prefer sour tastes much more than babies or adults do.

It's also true that our taste preferences can change from moment to moment because we enjoy a taste—even something we love—less and less with each bite. In an unexpected experiment, I lived through an example of "sensory-specific satiety" and its counterpart, the "buffet effect," at dinner one evening.

Jamie likes to cook, but when he's making dinner, he doesn't worry much about having everything ready at the same time. One night, he, Eleanor, and I sat around the table eating his meatballs, and after three meatballs, I said, "Wow, I can't eat another bite." At which point he pulled out a tray of roasted cauliflower, one of my favorite foods.

As I loaded up my plate, Eleanor said, "I thought you were full."

"I'm too full for more meatballs" (sensory-specific satiety), I said, "but I've got room for cauliflower" (buffet effect). For this reason, some restaurants present a series of small dishes, to keep the sense of reward high.

We can trick our taste buds. For fun, I popped a "miracle fruit" tablet into my mouth. Made from the berries of a West African shrub, the tablet contained a protein that, in the presence of acid, tricked my tongue to fire up the taste of sweetness. When I sucked on a lemon slice, it tasted like oversweetened lemonade, and when I bit into an unripe strawberry, it tasted like candy.

I also tried crunching Szechuan buttons, which made me feel as if I'd stuck an electric buzzer in my mouth. These "buzz buttons" stimulated my trigeminal nerve—the large nerve that also allows us to experience the astringency of red wine, the burn of chilies, and the cool of mint.

Our upbringing, our culture, and our values help us decide what to eat. Even in the least restrictive cultures, people don't eat all "foods" that are nutritious and available—some foods are considered acceptable, and others off-limits. Why will I eat cow but not horse? Why have I eaten a cow's muscle but not a cow's liver, which, not long ago, was a popular dish in the United States? I've never tried crickets, even though they're nutritious, environmentally friendly, and, I've heard, tasty. In general, if we haven't had a positive eating experience with a food by age twenty-five, we probably won't embrace it.

While our sense of taste dominates our experience of eating, the other four senses also make significant contributions. First, appearance matters. Back in the first century, the Roman gourmet Apicius noted, "The first taste is always with the eyes." The fiery orange of Cheetos tells our brains to expect a big hit of flavor, and steamed vegetables look more appetizing when they keep their bright colors. In the United States, we associate the color blue with salty, red with sweet, and green with sour; people rate popcorn as saltier when they eat from a blue bowl and as sweeter when they eat from a red bowl.

Sounds also influence how something tastes. Would an apricot have the same flavor if we didn't hear that soft squelching sound during a bite? In one study, people rated potato chips as fresher-tasting when they heard a louder crunch. In another study, people were asked to rate two (identical) wines, one poured from a corked bottle and one poured from a screw-capped bottle. When participants heard the pop of a cork being pulled, they gave the wine a higher rating—and they also rated it as more likely to spark a celebratory mood. And it's the snap, crackle, and pop that make Rice Krispies cereal fun to eat.

Smell, of course, is essential to a food's flavor. For that reason, prepared foods often don't taste as good as the foods we cook because we don't get the smells of roasting, caramelizing, grilling, or baking that would otherwise waft through the air to build our anticipation and boost the flavor of the meal.

When we're deciding whether something tastes good, we're also very influenced by its mouthfeel: soggy, crispy, creamy, silky, slimy, gristly, gooey, grainy, oily, spongy, fluffy, crumbly, crunchy, stringy. (I love the word *mouthfeel*: so clunky, so apt.) Different cultures appreciate different textures; for instance, East Asian and Southeast Asian cuisines embrace a far wider range of textures—including slippery, springy, rubbery, chewy—than those in Western cooking.

I experienced food's five-sensation delight one Sunday morning, when I walked into the kitchen to discover that Jamie was busy at the kitchen counter. I sized up the ingredients heaped on the counter.

"A frittata?" I guessed.

"Yep."

"Wonderful." I loved everything about Jamie's frittatas: the sharp pop and drifting scent of onions and red peppers as he sautéed them, the springy texture that melted in my mouth, the deep yellow and brown colors glistening in a round baking dish.

As he heated a skillet, I couldn't resist flicking some water onto its hot surface, to hear the sizzle—a sound, I'd only recently noticed, that I loved.

Later, as we all dug in, I said to Jamie, "You make the best frittata anywhere."

Sharing food is an ancient, universal, and revered human custom and is one of the most important expressions of community. Eating together is a way to strengthen relationships, and offering food is an essential ingredient of hospitality. In fact, we often eat foods we don't enjoy, or eat more or less than we'd like, out of respect or affection; for many people, sharing food means love.

Shared tastes are a crucial part of shared identity—within a culture and also within a family. I like certain foods, like tuna fish salad, chili, and stuffing, only when they're prepared the way my family makes them. (Other people add things like raisins or walnuts where they don't belong, and they don't understand that deviled eggs aren't improved by onions, and that meatballs should never contain chunks of mushrooms.) When we're sad or worried, we often turn to comfort foods—foods that, in our personal gastronomy, suggest peace and security.

Eating food satisfies our five senses, and so does preparing food. Every Christmas of my life, I've made gingerbread cookies with my family; buying gingerbread cookies wouldn't be the same. As acclaimed chef Carla Hall pointed out during an interview on the *Happier* podcast, "It's one thing to *break* bread together, it's another thing to *make* bread together."

I may not be a connoisseur of taste, but few things boost my happiness more than enjoying a meal with people I love.

Writing a Tastes Timeline

When writer Marcel Proust ate a tea-soaked madeleine cookie, he was famously flooded with memories of the past, and today the "Proust effect" refers to an intense, emotional memory sparked by the senses. However, while Proust's madeleine moment is often associated with the power of scent, Proust actually writes more about the *taste* of that famous madeleine.

As I reflected on my own taste memories, I immediately thought of Winstead's, a diner in Kansas City. I'm sure that I've sat in every booth, touched every plastic menu, and pulled napkins from every dispenser. When I was growing up, it was a treat to go whenever my mother didn't feel like cooking or when a day was particularly busy. I always order the same thing, though over the years I've graduated from a single Winstead burger, to a double Winstead, to a triple Winstead, without the bun.

Winstead's diner is an important symbol of our family identity and history: We're a family that loves Winstead's. Every time Elizabeth or I return to Kansas City, we eat at Winstead's on our very first day back, we always take a photo in front of its green neon sign, and we've taught our own families to love Winstead's. How many times have I heard my father say, "I'd like a double Winstead, please, with everything, no cheese"? And every time we dig in to those flat, lacy, spicy burgers, I feel the connections strengthen.

On my last visit, I swiped a menu as a souvenir.

Inspired by Proust and by Winstead's, I decided to gather my remembrances of tastes past in a timeline. To conjure memories, I tried to recall the tastes that were most typical (the food and drink that I most often tasted during that period) or most distinctive (the food and drink that I enjoyed at that time, and no other time).

Childhood:

- Winstead's burgers, fries, onion rings, and chocolate Frosties—Our family ordered, and continues to order, some combination of these items at every visit.
- Pop-Tarts—My sister and I loved Strawberry Pop-Tarts, but we were allowed to eat them only when visiting our grandparents.
- My mother's meatloaf—This meatloaf is still one of my very favorite foods. The secret ingredient is: no secret ingredient.
- My father's Swedish pancakes—Every time he makes them, he announces, "These taste just like the ones my neighbor Mrs. Bargel used to make when I was a boy." It makes me happy that the tastes of my childhood tie me back to my father's childhood.
- Golden Grahams cereal—This supersweet cereal was my school-day breakfast for years.

College and law school:

- White Russians—My roommates and I made these heavy, sweet drinks during freshman year.
- Rice pudding from Naples Pizza—I lived across the street from this favorite college hangout, which was famous for its rice pudding.
- Sangria and tortilla chips from Viva Zapata restaurant—Like all college students, we were always on the hunt for free food, and as long as we kept ordering pitchers of sugary, cheap sangria, we could ask for more chips.

- Greek salad from Yorkside Pizza—This salad features giant chunks of feta and extra black olives; I still order one whenever I'm in New Haven.
- Diet Peach Snapple—Of course.

My daughters' childhoods:

- Baby food—Every once in a while, I snuck a taste.
- Pepperidge Farm Goldfish—My daughters loved these cheery, orange, fish-shaped crackers.
- Cheerios—This O-shaped cereal was another favorite snack.
- "Healthy" apple muffins—I couldn't resist ordering these moist, dense muffins when I worked on my laptop in a coffee shop across from my daughters' preschool.
- Shredded-wheat cereal with salsa—The only dish I ever invented. I was looking for a vehicle for salsa that was healthier than tortilla chips, and I had the inspiration to use shredded-wheat cereal. While I admit it doesn't look appealing, it's *delicious*.

Today:

- Chaffle (cheese and egg waffle)—Every morning, I heat my electric waffle-maker, mix two eggs with shredded cheddar cheese, pour the mixture onto the patterned surface, close the lid, and after a few minutes, pull out my browned, crispy chaffle.
- Almonds—I eat a lot of almonds, raw and roasted, salted and unsalted.
- Cauliflower and broccoli—I never tire of cauliflower and broccoli, though I lean slightly in favor of cauliflower.
- Cobb salad—I usually don't eat mixed foods, but I do like Cobb salad.
- Frozen raspberries—I love raspberries, and they're easier to keep stocked when they're frozen.

Asking myself the specific question "What tastes do I remember from a particular time?" helped me to dredge up memories of scenes that I hadn't thought about for years. I didn't even need to track down these items to eat them; just recalling their tastes was enough.

I called Elizabeth to reminisce. "Remember all the Wheat Thins we ate in the car, whenever we took that daylong drive to North Platte?"

"Yes! Also Cheez-Its," she reminded me. "We always brought a box."

"What else do you remember?"

"Mom's pork chops. We ate those once a week, and I loved them, and I've never eaten a pork chop since."

"Oh, I remember those."

"And remember, when they visited, how Grandma and Grandpa would bring a coffee cake?"

"Yes, in the yellow tin." I hadn't thought about that old cake tin in decades, but it was right there in my memory. Then I started to laugh.

"You know what else I remember?"

"What?" asked Elizabeth.

"How much you loved butter!"

"I still love butter."

"You had that way of buttering Saltines, then putting them in the toaster oven to melt the butter. And then that one time the toaster caught on fire! We screamed for Dad, and he came and just *blew out* the fire, like the Big Bad Wolf."

"Well," Elizabeth admitted, "that may have happened more than once."

The nostalgia of recalling these tastes made me feel closer to my own past, and also closer to my sister, because these were memories that no one else shared. And in fact, research suggests that feelings of nostalgia can help people feel happier and less lonely.

Remembering the tastes of my childhood made me curious to hear about my daughters' taste-memories.

"Think back to when you were much younger," I said to Eleanor over a lunch of Jamie's latest specialty, an onion tart. "What tastes stand out?"

"For my birthday parties, we'd buy those big boxes of Froot Loops and red licorice whips to make Froot Loop necklaces," she said. "All my friends loved that."

"That was so fun," I said. "What else?"

"For a long time, I had chunky peanut butter on whole wheat bread for breakfast. Also, I ate a lot of raisins."

"Raisins?"

"Don't you remember how we had those jars of golden raisins? I'd eat them out of my special cup."

"I forgot about the raisins! Everything got sticky from the raisins."

Next, I called Eliza to ask about her memories and associations.

"When you went to college, what tastes did you miss most from home?"

"Parmesan," she said. "At home I can eat it at any time in any form." True. Thanks to Eliza, we keep many forms of Parmesan in the fridge at all times. "And," she added, "I remember how you used to make me warm milk when I had trouble falling asleep. When I was little, like six years old, I had so much trouble sleeping."

I had completely forgotten about the period when Eliza couldn't sleep, but then the memory of heating up her milk in the microwave, then adding vanilla and cinnamon, came back to me—and with it, the feeling of being the mother of young children, with its many sleepless nights.

In what's called the "reminiscence bump," adults tend to remember most vividly their experiences from between the ages of fifteen and twenty-five. By attending more closely to my five senses, I found that I was recalling more memories, from more times in my life.

These memories had been preserved, but I'd never thought about them; now that I was paying attention, they'd begun to surface. Revisiting old tastes made me happy but also wistful: So much in my life had changed, or vanished altogether.

As Proust observes, during his reflection about the taste of tea and cake:

> When from a long-distant past nothing subsists, after the people are dead, after the things are broken and scattered . . . the smell and taste of things remain poised a long time, like souls, ready to remind us, waiting and hoping for their moment, amid the ruins of all the rest; and bear unfaltering, in the tiny and almost impalpable drop of their essence, the vast structure of recollection.

Every time I return to Kansas City, I visit Winstead's, and I wonder: How can it have changed so little when so much has changed for me? Yet even if Winstead's closes its doors, I can remember those days every time I smell French fries.

Admiring Ketchup and Vanilla

As demonstrated by the fact that my favorite restaurant was a diner, I didn't have a very adventurous palate, but I realized that there was another way to find more joy in taste: I could cultivate more appreciation for the familiar tastes of my own kitchen. Just as I'd done with my sense of sight, I could look for what I'd overlooked. I decided to explore two familiar yet magnificent flavors, both so common and so cheap that they're discounted, and even disparaged, despite being wildly popular.

Those two flavors? Ketchup and vanilla.

First, tomato ketchup. People love the tomato, which is one of the most widely consumed foods in the world; wherever it has been introduced, people have added it to their cuisine. In the United States, the tomato is second only to the potato as a popular vegetable. (Despite the old trick question, the tomato can qualify as both a fruit and a vegetable, and the U.S. Department of Agriculture categorizes it as a vegetable.)

Scarlet, viscous, and delicious, ketchup is one of the most popular ways to consume tomatoes. Ketchup started in China, hundreds of years ago, as a fermented fish sauce called *ke-tsiap,* which eventually made its way around the globe to the United States, where tomatoes became an essential part of the recipe. Nowadays, about 650 million bottles are sold *each year,* and about 97 percent of Americans have a bottle in the refrigerator.

We don't give ketchup much thought, and many people even dismiss it as the condiment that undiscriminating eaters use to overpower the flavor of anything it touches. The flavor of ketchup, however, is exceptionally complex. Heinz ketchup is the rare food that has the magical ability to hit each of the five basic tastes: sweet, sour, bitter, salty, and umami. That span may explain why ketchup is well loved both as itself and also as the secret ingredient in many popular foods, such as chili, meatloaf, and stir-fries, and in many sauces and dressings, such as Bolognese sauce, barbecue sauce, sweet-and-sour sauce, Russian dressing, and Thousand Island dressing.

Still, ketchup retains its stigma. At a business lunch, a colleague mentioned that she was going to a Thai restaurant for dinner, and I told her, "Guess what I just learned! A main ingredient in American Pad Thai is *ketchup.* Pad Thai is basically 'noodles with ketchup.'"

She wasn't happy to hear it.

I thought I knew the taste of ketchup well, but after learning more about it, I decided to give it more attention. I pulled the bottle of Heinz ketchup from the refrigerator door, squirted a dollop onto a spoon, and put a little on my tongue. The ketchup did indeed hit all five tastes, and its aftertaste was just as good as the immediate explosion of flavor. Plus I admired ketchup's rich, shiny red color and its thick, flowing texture.

I tried to think of other five-taste wonders. My best answer was the margarita cocktail, with its combination of the salt on the rim of the glass, the sweetness of the agave syrup or orange liqueur, the sourness of the limes, and the bitterness of the tequila. No umami, though.

Online, I asked people for suggestions of more four- or five-taste foods, and they suggested many:

Apple pie with cheddar cheese
Sweet-and-sour pork
Pho, depending on what you put in it
Crackers with honey and a sharp cheese
Thai red curry
Worcestershire sauce
Tamarind fruit
Kitchari

I realized that we had one of these items in our cabinet. I poured a few drops of brown Worcestershire sauce into a spoon and gave a taste; sure enough, I could pick up sour, sweet, salty, and umami, though I wasn't sure about bitter.

Discovering the magic of ketchup (and Worcestershire sauce) made me eager to turn to my next taste subject. Vanilla—or, more precisely, vanilla extract—is something we keep in our kitchen at all times, and I use it just about every day.

I've always loved vanilla. Ironically, although the term *vanilla* is sometimes used to describe something bland and boring, vanilla is one of the most powerful flavors in the world.

We tend to think of it as the flavor in desserts like crème brûlée, tapioca pudding, vanilla ice cream, or vanilla wafers, but it's also often a component of flavors like chocolate, caramel, and coconut, because it balances sweetness, masks bitterness, adds creaminess, and makes everything taste better. In the West, our association of sweetness with vanilla is so strong that we can make something taste sweeter just by adding vanilla—even though vanilla itself is not, in fact, sweet. In East Asia, where vanilla is associated with savory foods, eaters don't experience this sweetening effect.

Learning about vanilla made me realize that although I love vanilla-flavored anything, I couldn't remember ever tasting vanilla itself. I headed to the kitchen, pulled out our bottle, and cautiously dabbed a drop onto my tongue. The scent drifting from the bottle was delightful; the drop on my tongue tasted of alcohol (alcohol carries the vanilla flavor), with a bitter kick that left a burn. And, it turns out, there was a reason that I didn't taste much: Vanilla has no taste at all. When we add a teaspoon of vanilla to a recipe, we're adding a pleasant smell, not a taste.

Surprisingly, I learned, we can enjoy a *lot* of vanilla. Most flavors taste good at a certain level but taste bad when more is added; vanilla keeps tasting good even at high levels. To test this feature of vanilla myself, the next time I spooned Greek yogurt into a bowl, instead of adding the usual three thin brown drops of vanilla, I poured in an overflowing tablespoon. I gingerly gave the yogurt a taste. Still good. (However, if I added a cup, I suspect that would be too much vanilla.)

Starting in the 1990s, vanilla even became a dominant ingredient in many perfumes, such as the blockbuster perfume Angel; one of my favorite perfumes is Tom Ford's Tobacco Vanille. In my fragrance class, I'd loved the smell of vanillin (think vanilla milkshake). While few scents and flavors are loved everywhere, admiration for vanilla seems to be fairly universal, maybe because breast milk has a suggestion of vanilla.

When I stopped to notice, the flavors of ketchup and vanilla became far more intense and enjoyable. I'd found my taste adventures without leaving my own kitchen.

Understanding How Tastes Differ

As we move through the world, our five senses flash us with cues about how and when to take action.

For the sense of taste, it seemed to me that I experienced more limited taste cues than other people did. I wasn't highly attuned to tastes, and I wasn't interested in exploring tastes. Through a writers' group, I'd met Reem Kassis, author of *The Palestinian Table* and *The Arabesque Table,* and hearing her describe her passionate interest in flavors and foods made me realize my own lack of attention.

"I always want to experience what I see, and I love to explore other cultures through taste," she told me. "Like when I was reading Chimamanda Ngozi Adichie's novel *Americanah,* I got interested in Nigerian cuisine, like jollof rice."

"So seeing people eat something makes you want to taste it yourself?"

"Yes. But I guess that's true for everyone. If you see or hear or read about someone crunching on a crispy chicken tender, something in your brain chemistry says, 'I need that now.'"

"That doesn't happen to me," I said.

"If you see people eating something, you don't want to try it?" she asked with surprise.

"Nope," I said. "It doesn't occur to me."

After this conversation, I mulled over our different responses. *Well,* I thought, *maybe I should accept the fact that I just wasn't very attuned to tastes.*

But then it hit me: Actually, I could be *excessively* attuned to tastes. I have a severe sweet tooth, with a love for cookies, candy, ice cream, breakfast cereals, and brown sugar straight from the box. Every year when I was growing up, we baked a German chocolate cake to celebrate my father's birthday. I distinctly recall thinking, *When I grow up, I'm going to make German chocolate cake, and I'm going to eat as much as I want from the batter, then the frosting, and then the finished cake.* I remember when Cookies & Cream ice cream hit the market, I couldn't believe how delicious it was. As Brillat-Savarin remarked, "The discovery of a new dish confers more happiness on humanity, than the discovery of a new star."

Most people like sweets, but for me, once I have the taste of something sweet in my mouth, I want *more, more, more,* in a way that makes me feel out of control: "Now, later; two, three, four; it's my birthday; it's special; right away; just a little; again."

More than a decade ago, I'd discovered that for me, there was a simple way to shape my sensory environment and conquer my sweet tooth.

I quit sugar.

I hadn't planned to quit, but in 2012, while on a family vacation, I happened to read Gary Taubes's book *Why We Get Fat and What to Do About It.* The book had caught my interest because it explored the crucial role of the hormone insulin in the body, and ever since Elizabeth had been diagnosed with type 1 diabetes, I'd wanted to learn more about insulin.

I read the book in two days and learned that many of the health problems spreading across the globe—such as cancer, type 2 diabetes, high blood pressure, and heart disease—can be traced to the quantity and quality of carbohydrates eaten, and a lot of those carbs are in the form of sugar. The in*toxic*ation of sugar is indeed toxic.

The book's argument struck me like a lightning bolt, and I decided to change the way I ate. Because we were staying at a hotel, I was able to switch my eating habits overnight, just by ordering different foods from the menu. With some uneasiness, that first morning, instead of getting my usual hotel breakfast of bran cereal, skim milk, and fruit salad, I ate scrambled eggs—with the yolks. From that day forward, I avoided sugar as well as other high-carb foods like grains and starchy vegetables.

From the start, I loved eating this way. I enjoyed the food. My blood work was excellent. I no longer felt ravenous between meals.

Best of all, I eliminated the boring, draining distraction of cravings; when I stopped eating sugar, I stopped wanting it. What a relief! Sometimes, by giving something up, we gain.

Our senses can give us a quick lift or a pleasant distraction, but we also sometimes succumb to the thrill of the senses in ways that aren't healthy. These days, for many people, it's hard to resist the impulse to indulge in a taste treat. For thousands of years, we humans have been cooking, boiling, grinding, grilling, and milling our food to make it safer, tastier, and more nutritious. In the past, however, we had to work much harder to gather our food, prepare our food, pay for our food, and even *chew* our food. Now food is ultra-processed to be irresistible, as food-industry experts engineer their products to hit the flavor "bliss points" that keep us coming back for more.

When I quit sugar, I learned that I'm an "abstainer"; when faced with a strong temptation, I do better when I abstain than when I try to indulge moderately. I can eat no Oreos, but if I eat one Oreo, I want ten Oreos. It's easier for me to have *none*. "Moderators," by contrast, fare better with moderation; when faced with a strong temptation, they do better when they indulge a little bit, or sometimes. A friend asked, "But where's the joy in life without the occasional brownie?" and I answered, "It's not true for everyone, but for me, not eating the brownie brings more joy than any brownie ever did."

People often told me, "It's impossible to quit sugar, because we encounter so many cues to indulge," so I'd always been puzzled by the fact that I'd found it so easy. I'd given up sugar (really, most carbs) overnight, and stayed clear of sugar ever since, without much effort. Given that my sweet tooth was so strong, why wasn't I constantly battling food cues from my environment?

At last, I figured it out. My five-senses investigation had taught me that brains don't report an objective set of facts; my brain tells me what *I* need to know, which is different from what other people need to know.

In the old days, I'd been tantalized by tempting smells wafting from a bakery or delectable rows of pastries lined up in a shop window. I couldn't ignore the containers of ice cream in our freezer. But as I thought about my present experience, I realized: *I almost never notice those cues of sweet fragrances or inviting sights.* Because I don't eat sugary foods, my brain and my senses have adapted and no longer press these messages on me—and so temptation drops away. Tastes differ, and taste worlds differ; it was startling to realize how different people's realities could be.

Nevertheless, if I wanted to, I could shape my experience by deliberately directing my attention toward whatever I wanted to appreciate. Fired up by Reem's enthusiasm, when I walked by the international food bazaar Essex Market in downtown Manhattan, I stopped in for the first time: I wanted to push myself to try something new. As I wandered through the wide aisles with their concrete floors, more exciting to me than the actual food was the atmosphere of *possibility* that the market held—the sense of the vastness of the world and its cultures and appetites. I particularly loved looking at the colorful mounds of fruits and vegetables and inhaling the fresh, earthy odor of plant life.

After weighing many options, I chose a container from a cooler and brought the unfamiliar food home to try.

"What are you eating?" asked Eleanor, when she walked into the kitchen as I was digging in.

"Seasoned pickled cucumbers," I read off the label. "Cucumbers, radishes, hot pepper powder. Want some? They're good."

"Pickled cucumbers?—I think you bought *pickles*," she said kindly.

"Really?" I said. "I tried so hard to make an interesting choice!"

Even when I tried to be adventurous, I didn't stray very far.

Comparing Tastes

To expand my limited appreciation for my sense of taste, I'd attended some tasting classes—including spending two days at FONA International's "Flavor University" in Illinois. Along with my seventy-five classmates, who were mostly flavor professionals, I learned how the body experiences flavor, how flavors were evaluated, and how the industry tracked the latest food trends. (Bottom line: Everyone wanted to discover the next Pumpkin Spice.)

My favorite exercises were the taste comparisons. I suspended my usual eating habits to try to discern the different tastes among types of applesauces, breakfast bars, milks, candies, and barbecue potato chips.

I decided to try some comparisons on my own, so one afternoon I stopped by the cheese section of a neighborhood gourmet grocery store. Other people had a tremendous appreciation for cheese, but I wasn't sure what types of cheese I preferred—or really, what did cheese even taste like? Overwhelmed by the variety, and intimidated by the sophistication of the conversation I overheard between a customer and the guy behind the counter, I grabbed practically the first cheeses I saw, some Gruyère and some goat cheese.

Back at my kitchen table, I first cut off a piece of the pale yellow Gruyère and popped it into my mouth. It was chewy, a little dry, with a salty, nutty taste and a slightly gritty texture; I felt the occasional satisfying crunch of crystals. I took a few more bites from sheer pleasure, sipped some water to reset my taste buds, and then turned to my other purchase.

As I bit into a thin slice of goat cheese, I noted that its edible rind was very satisfying to chew, and the cheese was much softer than the Gruyère, almost gooey. I liked the texture, but I was turned off by its earthy, tangy flavor.

I'd eaten both kinds of cheese before, but I hadn't paid enough attention to have a sense of them. Now I knew: I loved Gruyère, and I could skip the goat cheese.

A few weeks later, I tried the same process with olives. I liked olives, but I'd never bothered to try to figure out what kind I preferred. I bought a small container of "Festival Mix," and, at my kitchen table, sorted the olives by type. I took a moment to admire their appearance—shiny, smooth, with an elegant shape and vivid colors.

One by one, I chewed the olives and took notes. I'd always figured that olives tasted more or less . . . like olives, so I was surprised by the variety. I didn't like the sour aftertaste of the big Cerignola olives, though I did admire their iconic color; when we describe something as "olive green," we mean "Cerignola olive green." I didn't like the small, brown Niçoise olives, with their bitter flavor. I admired the bright shiny green of Castelvetrano olives, but they didn't offer a satisfying density. With an utter lack of originality, I decided that my favorite was that olive classic, the Kalamata. I liked its dark purple color, smooth skin, dense "meat," and rich, salty aftertaste.

When I paid close attention to sensations, my muddled impressions—"cheese" or "olive"—became clear and distinct. It reminded me of putting on my glasses and seeing my blurry surroundings snap into focus.

Also, making comparisons taught me about myself—what did I enjoy? Instead of assuming that if other people liked something, I liked it, too, I really considered my own preferences. The more I shaped my sensory world to reflect my individual tastes, the more enjoyable that world would be.

Plus the fun of making comparisons gave me an idea. Ancient philosophers and contemporary scientists agree that strong social ties are a key to happiness. Building relationships boosts happiness, lengthens life, strengthens immunity, and cuts the risk of depression, but it requires time and effort.

While I loved seeing friends, I rarely felt like inviting people over. Now I thought of a way to put a twist on the typical dinner party to create an event I'd be happy to host. Because sharing tastes was a great way to connect with people and get to know them better, I'd organize a taste party. Jamie liked the idea, so I invited two couples to an hour of taste sensations.

Before the guests arrived, I set up. I'd bought little cups and spoons, and I wrote "A," "B," or "C" on various cups, then distributed samples of the foods and beverages I'd selected. I chose a mix of natural and processed flavors, and I included items that would allow us to compare flavors, as well as a few exceptional items to discuss. (Again, in the spirit of scientific inquiry, I lifted my usual no-carb rule.)

As my friends took their seats, they each faced two plates with little cups filled with their array of tastes.

"I'll give you some particular tastes to try, and we'll also do some comparisons," I explained. "In the center of the table are some unsalted crackers, if you want to clear your palate between tastes, and also some filtered water. Let's start by comparing the potato chips. You have A, B, and C, so try A."

All six of us popped the A chip into our mouths and chewed for a moment. Then the debate started.

"Good flavor, does its job, and moves on."

"Yes, this is a great potato chip."

"No, it's too salty!"

"*Way* too salty."

"It's good but boring."

"That's the number one chip in the United States," I revealed. "Lay's Classic."

And, it turned out, around the table we all preferred the Lay's chips to 7-Eleven's in-house line of 7-Select Kettle Potato Chips (musty, oily) and the third-most-popular-in-the-U.S. Pringles (crispy, didn't taste like potato)—though Pringles did have a few outspoken fans.

Next, we compared raw almonds to raw cashews, and I was surprised by everyone's enthusiasm for the almond, with praise for its flavor, texture, and aftertaste. "An almond tastes better when you eat just one," a friend observed.

Next, we turned to two brands of milk-chocolate bar.

As soon as she started to bring the first piece of chocolate toward her mouth, one friend announced, "Hershey's!"

"How did you know?" I asked.

"That smell! It's unmistakable."

We agreed that the gourmet chocolate bar tasted smoother and creamier, but a few people found both bars too sweet. Not me. *I love sweet.*

The next cup had a little spoon sitting next to it. "This is ketchup," I explained. "Heinz brand, by far the most popular brand in the United States. Ketchup is remarkable because it contains all five tastes: sweet, sour, salty, bitter, and umami. So see if you can pick up all five."

Everyone gave a thoughtful taste to the tiny spoonful. Consensus: We all admired ketchup.

"I never eat ketchup. But it's good."

"It's a *rich* taste. The different flavors come out as you taste it."

"You see why people love it so much."

"If I hadn't known this was ketchup, I would've guessed that it was something expensive and sophisticated. It's so complex."

Good idea, I thought to myself. *The next time I do a taste party, I'll turn down the lights and ask people to try ketchup, to see if they can identify it.*

I thought it was time to try something unprocessed, so next we tried three samples of apples. As we compared, I read off adjectives meant to help us describe what we were tasting.

"Does it taste floral?" I suggested. "Astringent? Cooked, fresh, juicy, peely, sweet, winey?"

We chewed, and after much discussion, I revealed that we had sampled three of the most popular varieties of apple in the United States. "Our first slice was Gala, which is the most popular; our second slice was the number two variety, Red Delicious, and our third slice was Granny Smith, which is fourth." I was surprised that Granny Smith was so popular. For me, it was too tart. And the Red Delicious was slightly mealy.

"Red Delicious is what I ate as a kid," one friend reminisced. "Now, I almost never eat apples, but growing up, I ate one every single day, after school."

"So did I!" I said. "I'd come home, watch some TV, and eat an apple before starting my homework."

I couldn't wait to spring the next taste on my friends.

"Try this cup now," I said, holding up a cup with a golden-colored liquid.

"I'm immature enough not to want to drink something that looks like that," Jamie commented.

"Go ahead," I said, shooting him a look. "How do you like it, and what do you think it is?" Everyone took a sip, and the response was immediate.

"What *is* this?"

"No!"

"I do not like this at all."

"This tastes like medicine."

"It has a kind of sourness to it, and also a sweetness . . . and it's almost metallic."

"A weird fake berry?"

"Okay, no one likes it," I said, "but what do you think it *is*?"

No one could guess.

"Red Bull! It came on the scene in 1987, and apparently flavorists were astonished that people liked it. These days, every energy drink has to have that 'spiky' quality."

"It doesn't taste good," a friend observed. He took another sip. "But maybe it's interesting?"

"I agree," I said. "I keep wanting to taste it again."

As a gift for the evening, one couple had brought a pack of Pop Rocks, so we ended by tasting that remarkable candy. Just as when I was a child, I loved experiencing the contrast between seeing the candy "rocks" sit quietly in my palm and then feeling them crackling in my mouth.

During the course of the party, we talked about our responses to the different tastes, and I saw patterns emerge. Some people emphasized aftertaste, while others talked about aroma, texture, authentic flavor, or "refreshingness." A few people (like me) loved sweet, even at the highest levels, and others enjoyed a lot of sour.

What was most striking was how many memories were evoked by the tastes. We talked about what we'd eaten at holidays; we recalled former co-workers' habits and different countries we'd visited; we disclosed our likes and dislikes; we talked about the candy we ate during childhood.

"I like candy mostly for nostalgic reasons," one friend reflected. "I've never liked Necco Wafers very much—they're too chalky—but they remind me of my mother. She always kept them in the car, because it gets so hot in Boston in the summer, and they don't melt."

"That's why I still love Cherry Mash," another friend added. "It was a candy that I ate as a kid." This prompted a spirited debate about the merits of Cherry Mash.

Doing taste tests was tremendously fun. We weren't just socializing; we were sharing an experience, and it got us all laughing and talking, and it made me feel closer to everyone around the table. I knew that my sister had drunk pickle juice as a child, but with my friends, I had less opportunity to learn their preferences and memories. Our conversation felt unusually warm and intimate. Learning little details—one friend was sensitive to food texture, another disliked most fruits—somehow gave me a better sense of their natures.

As we were cleaning up, I asked Jamie, "Did you have fun?" He didn't naturally gravitate toward this kind of experience.

"I did—I think everyone did. It was different. Should we do it again?"

"Absolutely."

Next time, we could offer a tea or coffee tasting after dinner. Or we could serve barbecue, and have a taste-off among tomato-based, mustard-based, mayonnaise-based, and vinegar-based BBQ sauces. Or for dessert, we could serve different brands of vanilla ice cream, and let people compare to decide which one was most delicious. I started making a list of friends to invite.

Sharing Taste Memories

The taste party and my other experiments had shown me that I could use my sense of taste to draw closer to people and to memories. I wanted to do it again, but in a more meaningful, intimate way.

It occurred to me that taste could help me learn more about my mother-in-law, Judy. Over the years, beyond a few scattered memories she'd mentioned, I'd never heard her describe the tastes of her childhood. If we explored her tastes and recollections together, I could get to know her more deeply.

And I knew where we could go. Judy was raised eating traditional Jewish dishes and knew how to cook many of them herself. In New York City, the Lower East Side was home to many waves of immigrants, but it's best known as a center for Jewish immigrant culture and is still a place to get great Jewish food.

When I asked Judy if she'd be willing to take a tastes tour with me, she enthusiastically agreed, and then Eliza and Eleanor asked to come along. Jamie's parents live right around the corner from us—*right* around the corner, we don't even need to cross the street—so on a beautiful summer day, sunny but not hot, we came downstairs to meet Judy to go downtown together.

As we emerged from our building, we saw her heading toward us. Fit and energetic, she was wearing her favorite khaki pants and tennis shoes, ready for a long walk.

"I didn't eat breakfast," Judy said. "This food is filling. We need to pace ourselves."

"Yes, let's split things into four pieces," I said. "That way, we can taste more and not fill up too fast."

"Where will we start?" Eleanor asked.

"Yonah Schimmel's Knish Bakery on East Houston," I said, consulting my map. I'd often heard people talk about knishes, and I love saying the word *kuh-nish,* but I had no idea what they tasted like, or even what they *looked* like. We headed downtown to Houston Street, the northern boundary of the Lower East Side, to find out.

The four of us crowded in to Yonah Schimmel's small store to contemplate rows of knishes, which turned out to be dough stuffed with fillings such as potato, sweet potato, red cabbage, and mushroom. After some debate, we decided to split a vegetable knish, which looked like a giant biscuit with a top flecked with vegetables.

The tiny store didn't have seats, so we stood on the sidewalk and dug in to the pastry with our plastic forks. An outer cup of flaky pastry held mashed potatoes mixed with carrots, onions, string beans, and spices.

"It's good," said Eliza. "I love mashed potatoes."

"Yes, I taste potatoes," I said. "I can't taste any other vegetables."

"It's good, but it's heavy. It's not as good as what my grandmother used to make," said Judy. "Hers were smaller and lighter. They were made of phyllo dough over some kind of filling, like a savory cheese or chopped liver. Or they could be sweet, if she used sour cherries. Wonderful."

We continued down East Houston Street to Russ & Daughters, an "appetizing shop" known for its smoked fish, caviar, and bagels. We'd been the only customers in the tiny knish store, but here, we had to wait in a long, slow-moving line before stepping inside.

As we waited, I asked Judy, "Where was your family from?" I'd heard bits of family history over the years, but I didn't have a clear picture of which family members came from where—in Jamie's family, or in my own family for that matter.

"My grandmother came from Berdichev, in Ukraine. The story goes that my great-grandmother came from Moscow. Jews weren't supposed to live in Moscow, but she was a hairdresser with fancy clients, so she was allowed to be there."

Judy described what she'd eaten growing up in Philadelphia and Atlantic City. "My parents and I lived with my mother's parents, and my grandmother did the cooking," she said. "She was a terrific cook. She made her own strudel dough. Hot borscht and cold borscht. She rendered her own chicken fat, which was used in so many dishes. I always knew the holidays were coming when we'd keep a big fish in water in the bathtub, until she was ready to cook it."

"Was the fish *alive*?" Eleanor asked. "How long was it in there?"

"Alive, dead, I can't remember. But it was in the tub."

"Did your mother cook, too? Or you?" I asked.

"My mother helped sometimes, but what my grandmother made was so labor-intensive. Preparing something would be the project for the whole day. And I didn't get interested in cooking until I was an adult. We didn't keep kosher, so we didn't have to follow all those rules. We did something that I don't think other families did—every Friday night my aunt and uncle would come over, and we'd eat bagels and lox."

"What kind of bagels?" Eliza asked.

"Plain. They didn't have all the other kinds back then."

As our line inched toward the door, we found ourselves standing in front of a window display of many kinds of dried fruit.

"Somehow, dried fruit seems modern to me," I said, "although of course it's not."

"We ate a lot of dried fruit when I was a child," Judy said. "Stewed prunes! I remember that. The old people wanted them."

Finally we made it inside the store, where shelves and glass cases stood packed with varieties of cream cheese, smoked fish, lox, and bagels. We studied the menu that stood on the countertop in a plastic stand-up frame. Judy chose the sandwich for us to split—the "meshugge," with smoked salmon, sable, and sturgeon layered on top of cream cheese on a bagel. (The sandwich ingredients were traditional, but the names were contemporary—other sandwiches included the "yum kippered," the "fancy delancey," and the "shtetl.") I asked the clerk to slice the sandwich into quarters, which was fortunate because it was *big*. Russ & Daughters didn't have any seating, so again we stood in a circle on the sidewalk to eat our portions.

"This sandwich is so high, I can't get my mouth around it," I said, wiping cream cheese off my chin.

"I love it," Eleanor announced.

"It's good," I agreed. "So salty." As I chewed, I tried to distinguish among the ingredients, but I couldn't sort out the different tastes. But whatever tasted like what, it tasted good. I'd worried that the fish slices might feel slimy in my mouth, but they didn't; perhaps the thick, slightly sticky texture of the cream cheese and the bagel's chewiness prevented it.

"Would you say that the food we're eating today is like what you ate as a child?" I asked Judy.

Judy thought for a moment before answering. "Well, it's not much like what I had, but it's the same *kind* of food. So it does make me remember how we ate."

After we finished our sandwich quarters, I pulled out my map again.

"What's the next stop?" Judy asked.

"Economy Candy. Have you ever been there?" This was one place on the Lower East Side that Eliza, Eleanor, and I had visited many times. (I love everything about candy except eating it.)

"No, I've never even heard of it."

"It's really something," I said. "A store from another time."

As we continued down the street to turn onto Rivington, I felt a rush of love for New York City. So many tastes, faces, uniforms, packages, professions—so many lives under way, all here. I wanted to wander down every street and hallway, and open every door, and say "Again, again, again!" The city was *right here, right now,* all around me.

The four of us walked into Economy Candy, and I stood in the doorway for a moment to adjust to the explosion that met our eyes. Modern candy stores, like It'Sugar and Dylan's Candy Bar, are slick, pricey, organized, and stylish; Economy Candy is old-fashioned, cheap, and messy.

I walked down the aisles and lingered over novelty items like bacon mints and chocolate Band-Aids, and old-fashioned candy like Satellite Wafers and candy cigarettes. There was British candy, Star Wars–themed candy, chocolate-covered anything, and every color of M&M's. I spotted Candy Buttons—those Damien Hirst–ish round candies attached to paper strips. They taste terrible, but I admired them as the color chart of candy.

"All this candy from the past!" Judy said. "I remember it."

"What was your favorite candy growing up?" I asked.

"Mary Janes," Judy said. "I'm looking for them now."

"I remember Mary Janes," I said. "Peanut butter– and molasses-flavored, so chewy."

After the clerk rang up our purchases, we continued down Essex to Grand Street. After stopping at Kossar's Bagels & Bialys to try a chocolate babka and a baked bialy sprinkled with onion flakes, we made our final stop at the Pickle Guys. The one-room store, which smelled salty and sour, was packed with forty red barrels brimming with pickled items—pickled okra, celery, carrots, beets, turnips. In spite of much deliberation, I opted for a container of whole dill pickles, and then we headed home.

Once we were back on our block, we said goodbye to Judy. "This was great!" she told us. "It was different from just going to a neighborhood and trying a bunch of different dishes. This really brought back memories. It was comforting to eat those old foods."

All four of us enjoyed our outing. We'd spent time together. We'd learned about Judy's experiences as a child, and through that,

Eliza and Eleanor had learned more about their family's past. We'd explored a historic area of New York City, and we'd had an adventure.

"That was great," Eliza said at dinner. "I'm glad we went."

"Why, exactly?" I asked.

"Well, I'd heard some stories about Grandma's childhood, but I didn't know all those details, like the fish in the bathtub. And we heard more about *her* grandmother—even though we know her grandmother was really important to her, Grandma never talks about her much. Plus I liked the food."

"It made it easier for me to picture Grandma as a child, what her life was like," Eleanor said. "It feels more real."

All a tribute to the power of the sense of taste.

Making the Daily Visit

To enhance my daily visits to the Met, I was determined to use each of my five senses. Fortunately for my sense of taste, the Met had a cafeteria and cafés as well as galleries.

Although these eating places were crowded and popular, they could seem like illegitimate add-ons: Weren't we supposed to spend our time looking at *art*? But the fact is, we may get hungry or thirsty, and even if not, we like to eat and drink, or we just need to take a break. Sometimes, to keep going, we have to allow ourselves to stop.

When I visited the Met with friends or family, I often suggested getting a drink or snack. When Eleanor and I visited together, we often stopped for lattes in the American Wing Court; it was so pleasant to sit in a beautiful place and enjoy a hot drink.

When I came to the Met by myself, however, taste was the least activated of my five senses. For one thing, I didn't want to take a break; being at the Met *was* my break. For another, while at home I often reached for something to eat or drink when I felt bored, at the Met, I embraced those moments of boredom.

Philosopher Gaston Bachelard wrote, "There are children who will leave a game to go and be bored in a corner of the garret. How often have I wished for the attic of my boredom when the complications of life made me lose the very germ of all freedom!" The Met was my attic. Through boredom, I found interest in rooms that, at first glance, looked dull. I learned to like the quirky expressiveness of ancient Cypriot statuettes, and I was amused by the fact that in the corner of a sumptuous French period room, next to a gilded harp, sat a velvet-covered, silk-lined dog kennel.

On one visit, just for something to do, I visited a marble sculpture from the site of the Eleusinian Mysteries. I've long been intrigued by the Eleusinian Mysteries; for hundreds of years, people traveled to Eleusis in Greece for a nine-day initiation that culminated in the revelation of a great secret. What fascinates me is that even though countless people were initiated over centuries, *no one ever betrayed the secret*. Even today, all we know is there were "things recited, things shown, and things performed."

As I gazed at the marble relief of the goddesses Demeter and Persephone standing with a boy, I reflected on this aspect of human nature. Whether it's a speakeasy, a gossip session, an Agatha Christie novel, a friend's medicine cabinet, research into the origins of the universe, or the Eleusinian Mysteries, we want to learn the secret.

I reflected, "Keeping information secret unfailingly makes it more interesting." That would make a good aphorism, I thought. I love aphorisms, which are short statements that contain large truths. "In fact," I realized with sudden excitement, "I could write my own collection of aphorisms." I would *love* to write a book of aphorisms.

For most people, writing a book wouldn't sound like play. But I often played hooky from my regular writing by working on unofficial projects—"My Color Pilgrimage," "The Oracle," "Almanac of Happiness"—for fun. (Sometimes my hooky books turned into real books, such as my once-hooky book *Outer Order, Inner Calm*.)

In the past, I'd worried that goofing off derailed my energy from my "real" projects. Was I just *procrasti-creating*—that is, delaying my work on a major project by fooling around with a side project? After all, working is one of the most dangerous forms of procrastination.

Time and experience, though, showed me the value of this play. As research confirms, the more we create, the more likely we are to create something worthwhile. The more trial, the more error—and also the more accomplishment. For me, it turned out, one way to get into this playful, productive frame of mind was to focus on my senses.

To keep pace with my racing thoughts, I began to stride through the galleries, where every object seemed to stand out in bold colors. Yes, I decided, I would absolutely write a book of aphorisms! I couldn't wait to get back to my desk to start a new document.

Lifting Taste by Dropping Sight

One of the most intriguing things I'd learned about the five senses? When one sense is diminished, our other senses work to fill the gap.

I'd been looking for a way to test this phenomenon when I heard about "Dinner in the Dark." Twice weekly, the downtown restaurant Abigail's Kitchen offers a dinner where guests sit blindfolded throughout a meal. "Without sight, diners' other senses are heightened," the website promises. "Smells, texture and sounds all become more intense."

I couldn't wait to try it, so I found a date when Eliza, Jamie, and I could go (the experience included wine, so underage Eleanor couldn't join us). On the appointed evening, along with thirteen other diners, we waited in the restaurant's bar area for the adventure to begin. "This seems to be a popular date-night activity," I observed, looking at the other people in line.

"Are you going to eat carbs, Mom?" Eliza asked.

"I'm going to eat whatever we're served. Bring it on!"

First, Abigail herself handed out lightweight adjustable masks that allowed us to open our eyes without being able to see. Group by group, we walked down a steep flight of stairs, put on our masks, and were led into the dining room to take our seats. I tried to imagine my surroundings. A recording of birds twittering was playing, which led me to imagine a garden décor, with a white-and-green color scheme, lattice patterns, and plants. (All completely inaccurate, I later discovered.)

As we settled in, Abigail directed us to find the little baskets in front of us and clean our hands on the warm washcloths inside. Then the servers gathered the washcloths, and the meal began.

The menu was secret, so Jamie, Eliza, and I had fun trying to identify what foods we were eating. The first taste was easy: a small triangle of crispy toast with olive oil, garlic, and plenty of salt. With our masks on, we really heard how much noise we made as we crunched.

Next was cold soup, served in a cup—delicious. We guessed that it was tomato with basil. The next course of cold pasta salad, with beets and goat cheese, was easier to identify. In the dark, I really noticed the pasta's smooth, firm surface, the beets' dirtlike sweetness, and the creamy texture of the goat cheese—fortunately, the cheese was mild, because as I'd learned from my taste test, I didn't enjoy a strong goat cheese.

"Do you think people sneak peeks during the dinner?" Eliza asked.

"Oh, absolutely."

The next course was served, and after a few bites of a rich, fatty, chewy meat, we decided we were eating steak, but none of us could identify the other, slightly tart flavor we were picking up.

"I'm having trouble cutting the food and getting it into my mouth," I said. "Are either of you finding it hard to get anything on your fork?"

"Me too," said Eliza.

"I've been using my hands a bit," I admitted. "Now we know why we needed those washcloths."

"It doesn't matter, no one can see you," Jamie said.

"The servers can see!" Eliza said. "Don't be gross!"

After an easily identified dessert of warm molten chocolate cake with vanilla ice cream, Abigail told all of us to remove our masks. When I pulled mine off, I saw that we sat in a cozy room, with light wood and a minimalist feel, which was very different from what I'd imagined. As Abigail revealed what we'd been eating and drinking, with each item, everyone laughed and exclaimed, "Oh, *that's* what it was!" We learned that the soup had been pea with mint, the entrée had been duck, and that tart flavor had been pomegranate. After her explanation, we all applauded, and the evening was over.

The dinner had been a terrific exercise in my sense of taste. I ate more slowly and paid more attention to each bite—its flavor and texture, and even the challenge of getting it to my mouth. I was far more aware of the different ingredients and spices that contributed to each dish.

The evening also turned out to be an exercise in other senses, as well. The small room was noisy with music and conversation—maybe to help us concentrate on eating?—so it was a little hard to hear, and because I couldn't see Jamie and Eliza, I had to listen more closely. Also, I kept reaching out to touch them both, as a way to stay oriented. It was an interesting mix of engagement: I felt both more connected to Jamie and Eliza, and less connected.

Best of all, the evening was *fun*—an elevated version of my own taste party. Jamie, Eliza, and I had a great time on an unusual adventure.

Considering the evening as an exercise in pure taste, however, I think I would've appreciated the flavors more if I'd known what I was eating. In her after-dinner talk, Abigail had noted that when making their reservations, many people included long lists of items they didn't want to eat. She'd explained that the eye mask wasn't meant to trick us into eating foods that we'd otherwise avoid but rather to help us pay attention to nonvisual aspects of dining. For me, while the mystery was fun, my wariness distracted me from enjoying my sense of taste.

The greatest pleasure of Dinner in the Dark, besides its novelty, was the chance to share a memorable evening with people I loved. Also, it made me realize that I usually didn't pay much attention to a dish's individual ingredients; I experienced it as having one combined flavor. During Dinner in the Dark, the lack of sight had led me to notice the various elements of each dish—in particular, I'd registered the saltiness level and the texture of each dish far more acutely than usual—and this greater refinement of sensation gave me more pleasure.

"From now on," I announced to Jamie and Eliza, "especially whenever I order something from a restaurant, I'm going to read the description of what's in it and really try to appreciate all the different ingredients."

"That's a good idea," Eliza said. "I'm going to try to do that, too."

The more we notice, the more we can enjoy.

Tasting More

As I prepared to leave the subject of "taste" for "touch," I recognized deeper changes in myself.

I'd first felt a shift on my unforgettable walk home from the eye doctor's office, when I'd been startled into a new awareness of my senses.

Now, even when I was doing everyday activities unrelated to my official five-senses experiment, I was flashing into sensation-focused mode. I noticed the woody, glassy scent of a liquor store; I listened to "Here Comes the Sun" as it played over a bookshop's loudspeaker; I picked up the faint taste of lime as I took a bite of avocado salad.

I was astonished to realize how much sensation I'd ignored in the past. I had assumed that I *couldn't* ignore it—because what could be more obvious than what I liked and disliked? But although my tongue had tasted or my eye had seen, my mind hadn't paid attention. Now

I knew I liked Kalamata olives but not Niçoise; I liked broccoli more than broccolini. I took an odd pleasure in watching as a pair of wipers swept rain from a car's windshield, I preferred the scent of rose to tuberose, and I really noticed when we switched to a new brand of paper towels.

My experience of my life—and my own nature—was growing clearer, more pronounced. The more I tried, the more I wanted to try.

In fact, in my eagerness to explore, I caught myself violating a social convention. I was at a lunch meeting with someone I didn't know well. His order came with a side of zucchini chips, which crunched loudly as he ate them. Before I thought better of the idea, I said, "Those chips you're eating sound so crispy and loud! They must be delicious! Can I try a few?"

"Sure," he said with an air of surprise.

As he spooned some zucchini chips onto my plate, I realized that I'd done two quasi-rude things: I'd acknowledged that he was making a lot of noise as he ate, and I'd asked someone I didn't know well to share food with me.

"Thanks, these are wonderful!" I said sheepishly. Oh, well.

As I reflected on my relationship to taste, I had to admit that while my life had become so much, well, *sweeter,* once I gave up sugar, it was also true that quitting sugar had deprived me of some fun. I never surprised my kids with cookies or ordered dessert for the table. Sugar does make food more exciting—would Adam and Eve have been tempted by a forbidden cabbage?

For me, renunciation was perhaps too easy. As writer Samuel Johnson observed, "Life is barren enough surely with all her trappings; let us therefore be cautious how we strip her." In part, I'd started my five-senses experiment to counteract my monk-like inclinations. I wanted a life without sugar, true, but I also wanted a life with more salt, more songs, more scarlet.

As I pushed myself to engage more deeply with my sense of taste, I realized that, even for me, it had superpowers. Taste (or really, flavor and food) tied me to the present moment—and it connected me to memories from the past. Going forward, I planned to pay more attention to these connections. Instead of vaguely registering that Jamie ate a lot of fudge during our weekend in Maine, I could make fudge a vehicle for a happy memory. In the future, in the middle of winter, I could bring home a bag of fudge for Jamie and say, "Remember the summer when we stayed in that little seaside town, and you ate so much fudge?"

Also, taste could help me deepen relationships, the way I'd grown closer to my mother-in-law by hearing about the foods of her childhood and learned more about my friends by debating our likes and dislikes. I'd started asking my friends—and even people I'd just met—questions about their taste histories: "In grade school, what did you eat for lunch?" "What favorite junk food did your parents refuse to buy?" "Did you have a great regional hometown food that you can't find anywhere else?" "What was your drink of choice in college?" "What food did you once enjoy that you now dislike, or vice versa?" People enjoyed reminiscing, and I got a glimpse into their lives.

Now that I appreciated its power to heighten the moment, evoke the past, and strengthen bonds, I understood why so many memories and traditions revolve around taste—and I resolved to give more attention to taste-based associations. Instead of absent-mindedly noticing that blueberries and fruit-flavored sorbet always reminded me of my father-in-law, Bob, or that the soft drink Fresca always reminded me of my friends from my book group, I would use these associations to remind me of deep bonds and, when I wanted to, invoke them deliberately.

Even more important, I would work hard to preserve taste-based traditions—like eating ice-cream cake for Jamie's birthday or sweet potatoes every Thanksgiving—because these traditions weren't just fun, they helped hold our family together.

And I'd never take ketchup for granted again.

Touching

○ ⑽ ⑦ ⑧ ⋀

My Brain Out on My Fingers, or
Why Holding This Stone Is Lucky

My lab is the place where I put my brain out on my fingers and I do things.
—HOPE JAHREN, *Lab Girl*

UNFORTUNATELY FOR HIM, JAMIE HAS A LOT OF BAD DREAMS. Not just the ordinary, uncomfortable kind of bad dreams—I often dream that I can't find my glasses—but real nightmares. He wakes up sweaty and drained. One morning, I saw him standing in our bedroom doorway when I came out of the bathroom. He held out his arms to me.

"Bad dream?" I asked, as I stepped in close.

"Oh, yes."

"Well, let it float away," I said, as I tightened my arms around him and put my head on his shoulder. We just stood there, silent, for a long time. I breathed in his familiar smell, a scent that I loved, strongest every morning just before he took his shower. I didn't say anything, and just gently ran my hands across his warm back as I tried to comfort him.

Then he gave a deep sigh and said, "All right."

Sometimes, words only diminish what we want to convey.

I COULD IMAGINE A LIFE without sight, sound, smell, or taste, but it seemed impossible to strip out my sense of touch. While seeing is believing, to *touch* feels like an encounter with the final reality. According to Catholic tradition, only touching Jesus's wound convinced the doubting apostle Thomas that Jesus had been resurrected.

When I began to investigate touch, I'd assumed that, for me, touch was a background sense along with hearing and taste. In fact, I came to realize, I was very sensitive to touch—somehow, I'd never noticed this fact about myself before.

I'd never registered how much I liked to stroke a velvet pillow, to pull the eggshell off the slick surface of a hard-boiled egg, to press my hand against a cool, damp, springy bed of moss, or to run my fingers gently over Eleanor's long, heavy hair. I couldn't pass a cactus without wanting to test its spines. I loved getting a massage (I felt like a puppy paying someone to scratch behind my ears). Because I wasn't allowed to touch the art in the Met, during my visits I'd find objects that I could touch, like the smooth wood of a bench or the cold metal of a staircase handrail.

Touch is different from the other four senses. While the sense organs of eye, ear, nose, and tongue are all part of the head, skin covers the whole body. Also, while my eyes are for seeing, and my ears are for hearing, my skin seems more like . . . packaging.

I rarely thought about my skin but, like just about every part of the body, it was wonderfully designed. Skin is one of our largest organs, weighs eight to fifteen pounds, when spread out is almost the size of a twin mattress, and is flexible and selectively permeable. It takes many forms: thickest on the heels, thinnest on the eyelids (which are 20 percent transparent so morning light can help our internal clock stay calibrated), and both hairy and smooth. In some areas, the skin can pick up very faint sensations, while in others, it registers only vague impressions. And at various entry points, like a Möbius strip, my *outside* flips *inside*.

The skin holds the many types of touch receptors that collect information from all over the body to send to the brain, in a complex, multilayered system of specialized detection. Areas like the lips and fingertips are far more sensitive than an area like the back, because they contain more receptors, more densely packed.

These layers of receptors are sophisticated enough to help us to feel pleasure, steer clear of pain, avoid drastic temperature changes, detect an itch or vibration or stretch, perceive texture, and bolster other senses. For touch, our hands are our most sensitive body part, followed by the lips and tongue. Sex organs are a source of great pleasure not because of their sensitivity—which refers to the ability to make very fine discriminations—but because of the way they're wired into the brain's reward circuitry.

All five senses are particularly alert to change, and that's true for touch: When information becomes predictable, it fades out of awareness. I jump when a spider crawls across my ankle, but I can't tickle myself. My favorite wool hat feels tight when I pull it on, but the feeling soon recedes.

The sense of touch can replace or supplement other sensory information. A sidewalk's strip of gridded bumps warns a pedestrian where the sidewalk leads into the street. A bed-shaker alarm clock wakes a sleeper by using vibrations instead of sound. These days, "haptics," or using technology to engage users through the sense of touch, has become a major area of development. Like a butler clearing his throat, my smart watch gives a polite shake to remind me of an appointment; a video game's handheld controller vibrates to make a virtual explosion feel more real.

And touch can make an object more enjoyable. Of our many

mismatched coffee mugs, the tall brown-and-white-striped mug is my favorite because it feels so good in my hand. It's not too heavy, not too light; warm but not hot after I've poured in my coffee; with a smooth glaze over shallow ripples along its sides. Years ago, my father-in-law, Bob, was reluctant to give up his BlackBerry because he preferred the feeling of pushing physical buttons to touching a flat screen.

Although we touch with our whole bodies, our hands play a unique role. To portray a person, we use the face—and if not the face, the hand. Some of the earliest surviving man-made images are stencils of hands on rock walls. These days, our fingerprints and our handwriting identify us, and when we use emojis, we're likely to use symbols of a face or hands to communicate our thoughts. We want "all hands on deck," or, in a more contemporary synecdoche, we schedule an "all-hands" meeting.

We explore the world with our hands. "Cease to use your hands," writer George Orwell noted, "and you have lopped off a huge chunk of your consciousness." There's a big difference between a zoo and a petting zoo. I can't look at a tree stump without wanting to rub my fingers across it, and I think food tastes better when I eat with my hands. Store clerks, teachers, and the parents of young children know how much we love to touch—and so do museum guards. One day at the Met, I was shocked to see a visitor running his hand across the smooth, dark stone of the monumental Sarcophagus of Harkhebit—should I tell the guard?—but I also felt sympathetic. I'd felt that urge myself. Every time I looked at the Yup'ik mask depicting a human hand holding a bird, a fish, and a seal, I itched to touch the wood frame.

Our hands inspire ingenuity and creativity. As writer and monk Yoshida Kenkō observed, "If we pick up a brush, we feel like writing; if we hold a musical instrument in our hands, we wish to play music." For me, a keyboard makes me want to write. We live in a digital age, of two kinds of digits: digital information and typing with our fingers.

The love of exploring with our hands is a big part of the appeal of visiting a store. Ordering online saves time, but for many people, touching is what makes shopping interesting. Cunning marketers tempt us to touch, because if we hold a product in our hands, we're more likely to choose it, and may even pay more for it.

One day, as I was reorganizing our massive collection of picture books, I pulled out *Pat the Bunny*, the 1940 classic by Dorothy Kunhardt. Slowly turning its battered pages, I felt the same pleasure I'd felt as a child as I patted the bunny's soft "fur," lifted the little sheet of smooth fabric, felt Daddy's scratchy face, and put my fingers through Mummy's ring. Even as a four-year-old, I'd realized that *Pat the Bunny* was different from other books because of the way it expanded past the page's usual visual limits.

Now I wanted to get more in touch with touch.

Giving a Loving Touch

Of everything that touch does, one of its most important functions is to help us engage with others. When she was little, Eleanor insisted on holding my hand whenever we walked together, and she'd frequently give my hand a quick kiss. The feeling of her small warm hand in mine is one of my favorite memories from those days.

Many people feel a strong desire to touch and be touched, and in particular, babies don't develop properly without touch. Babies who get skin-to-skin contact gain weight more quickly, sleep better, cry less, and get fewer infections; when they don't receive social touch, they can suffer terrible consequences. Many babies raised in the woefully understaffed Romanian orphanages in the 1980s and '90s showed slowed growth and behavioral and cognitive issues.

Because she was born early, Eliza spent a week in the hospital before coming home. Each morning, amid the beeping monitors, harsh hospital smells, and bustling nurses, I sterilized my hands and arms, picked her up from her incubator, and cuddled her against my bare stomach. I rocked her for endless hours, with all my attention focused on her tiny, warm body—so small that even her name felt too big for her. And in some mystical way, I did feel that I was pouring my energy into her through my loving touch.

For adults as well, human touch may help to lower stress, blood pressure, and pain; boost our immune system and mood; and help us to sleep better. Because being touched by another person releases natural painkillers in the brain, touch practices like massage have long been associated with health, comfort, and pain relief. For my birthday, I got an electric body-massage pillow. I enjoyed feeling it knead into the small of my back or against my shoulders—but it didn't feel nearly as good as being touched by a person.

Not only do we benefit from human touch, we grant it special powers. The "laying-on of hands" to convey blessing or healing is a widespread custom. For instance, in Europe in the Middle Ages, the "royal touch" was thought to cure scrofula. The Hindu spiritual leader Amma, known as the "hugging saint," blesses people through her hug.

Appropriate touch helps to foster feelings of gratitude, trust, and sympathy. When we're touched by doctors, we tend to rate them as more caring—and we even have better medical outcomes. In my neighborhood, I often see construction workers talking and drinking coffee before their workday begins. I remember one group where, as new crew members arrived, each quickly shook the hands of everyone already gathered. It seemed like such a good way to create a feeling of respect and connection among people who worked together.

But while touch can be beneficial, it can also be harmful. Inappropriate and unwanted touch can be intensely distressing and outright illegal, so we learn the importance of respecting boundaries and erring on the side of restraint. Cultures vary dramatically in how much people touch one another, and even within a culture, people have different levels of comfort with hugs, slaps on the back, and how closely people should stand together. For this reason, touch is increasingly discouraged in many contexts in the United States, which perhaps helps account for the popularity of services such as airport massage, chiropractors, and manicures. They allow us the comfort of touch in controlled, socially acceptable ways.

To state the obvious, loving touch can be a vital aspect of close relationships. As a true Midwesterner, however, I wasn't raised that way. The atmosphere of my family has always been very loving, but we don't show affection through touch. For instance, these days, my parents, Elizabeth, and I give a brief hug at the beginning of a visit and an equally brief hug to say goodbye, and rarely give one another a touch in between.

With Jamie, I've learned to touch far more often, because while Jamie may not seem like a big softie at first meeting, he is. He loves romantic comedies, he gives very thoughtful gifts, he frequently says "I love you," and he loves holding hands, giving a long hug, and linking arms.

After I learned about the science behind the power of touch—and also because I knew how important touch was to Jamie—I decided to try to tap into it more deliberately to help us feel closer to each other. When we walked Barnaby in the morning, I'd take his hand or put my arm through his arm, and I made sure that each hug was a real embrace, not just some perfunctory squeeze.

I also used touch to soothe the inevitable irritations we felt with each other. For instance, I made a point of harnessing touch whenever we needed to have a tough conversation.

"We need to go over some complicated scheduling questions," I told him one evening.

"Can't we do it later?" he asked.

"We've been putting this off. It's a drag, but let's just do it."

"Fine."

As we pulled out our calendars and began the annoying task of juggling logistics, I put my hand on his back. Usually these kinds of discussions put us in bad tempers, but the physical connection helped us keep the conversation light and warm. I added a new item to my Manifesto for Listening: "If appropriate, give a touch during a tough conversation."

I also started to go out of my way to create more moments of everyday physical connection among our family. Ever since I'd done my first happiness project, I'd aimed to "kiss more, hug more, touch more." Now I decided to redouble my efforts to give two big hugs each day to each family member. A good-morning hug, a welcome-home hug, a good-night hug, a you're-the-best hug, an I-hope-you-feel-better-soon hug—every day offered at least two natural opportunities for hugs. My favorite kind of hug, though, was our traditional all-family hug. Every once in a while, I'd yell, "Family love sandwich!" and we'd all crowd together to make one big hug.

No surprise, this kind of frequent, full-body, warm contact made us feel closer to one another. If we were having a moment of tension, our hug defused it; if we were having fun, our hug prolonged it.

What's more, the benefit of social touch isn't limited to the touch of another person. The loving, warm touch of an animal can provide tremendous comfort as well as improvements in health—for instance, one study showed that a ten-minute encounter with a therapy dog helps lower patients' pain during their time in the emergency room.

Our dog, Barnaby, made us happier in many ways, and one way was through physical contact. Jamie loved to sit with Barnaby nestled on the sofa beside him. At first Barnaby slept in his crate, but at some point, we decided to let him sleep wherever he wanted. I was surprised by how comforting (although sometimes uncomfortable) it was to have a dog sleep at the foot of our bed.

Reaching Out for Comfort and Delight

The touch of a person or animal isn't the only way we can find comfort and delight in touch.

For instance, most of us could use more tools for managing anxiety. Like all emotions, anxiety has value: It nudges me to schedule a checkup, proofread my draft for typos, and save for retirement. But anxiety can also be a distracting and destructive force, and our sense of touch can help us manage it.

Children turn to stuffed toys and soft blankets for solace—and so do adults. My sister Elizabeth still sleeps with her tattered Blankey. A friend told me, "My aunt works in palliative care, and she told me they recently put in a big order for light, cuddly throws. It's really comforting for people to hold on to something soft and warm."

A weighted blanket is another popular touch tool. Though there's not much research to prove that they work, some people find that weighted blankets help them feel less anxious and sleep better. When my daughters were babies, I'd seen how tight swaddling helped them to calm down, so I bought a weighted blanket and used it a few times. It didn't do anything for me, but Jamie and Eleanor like pulling it over themselves. Especially when he wasn't feeling well, the blanket helped Jamie to fall asleep. As I considered this difference in our responses, I thought, "No tool fits every hand." (Then I thought: aphorism!)

Habits such as nail-biting and knuckle-cracking give us something to do with our hands—which I understood well, because I was a lifelong hair-twister. Coiling my hair around my finger, then pulling, was deeply satisfying and helped me calm down and stay focused. But as much as I love to twist my hair, for the last several years, I'd been trying to resist because, as a left-handed twister, I had broken hair on the left side of my head. But what could I do instead?

As I was considering this problem, and exploring the power of touch, I happened to read actor Andrew McCarthy's memoir *Brat: An '80s Story*. During the filming of the movie *St. Elmo's Fire*, McCarthy was anxious about performing in a demanding, intimate scene. At the last minute, he grabbed a set of bongo drums to play on set. He observed that while some actors disliked working with props, he found them invaluable: "A cup of coffee, or a watering can . . . help to ground the work and take the internal focus away from the self and place it on behavior, liberating the performance." Playing the bongos allowed him to excel in that scene.

After reading this observation, I realized that in demanding situations, I used a prop myself. Sometimes I twisted my hair—and sometimes I held a pen. Whether I was in an important meeting, in a social situation like a party, or just sitting at my desk, I found a reason to hold a pen in my hand. It just felt good.

When I asked, I discovered that many people used props to help them manage anxiety and to concentrate. A friend told me, "At work, I'll roll a piece of Scotch tape between my fingers. At the end of the day, those balls are all over my desk."

I asked online for more examples and received many thought-provoking responses:

> I'm a brand photographer for wine, and my subjects—winemakers, vineyard managers, and crews—are more comfortable when they have something to hold when being photographed. I give them a glass of wine or some other prop.

> I hold a clipboard to stay calm when running events.

> I struggle with anxiety during appointments, meetings, and conversations, particularly when the focus is on me. I try to have a water bottle handy filled with ice-cold water. When I feel anxious, I feel hot, red, and like I'm not in my body, having something cold to hold on to helps me feel more grounded.

Several teachers mentioned holding a mug as a prop while teaching, and I was particularly struck by one teacher's solution:

During the pandemic, I had to teach via video, which made me anxious, and one day I grabbed a polished stone that was near my desk, and it made all the difference. The smoothness, the heft, the opportunity to shift it from hand to hand really calmed me down. I made sure I had that stone ready before every class, along with all my tech stuff.

Another teacher discovered a useful tool for a struggling student:

I had to remind one student to refocus multiple times a day. Then I found Calm Strips, stickers with a bumpy surface that you can rub or pick at. We put some on his laptop, and he found that rubbing them while he listened to the lesson helped him keep his focus. I also gave some to my adult daughter who has anxiety, and she found them very soothing.

Intrigued, I ordered packs of "Soft Sand" and "River Rocks" Calm Strips. I kept them on my desk, and I was surprised by how often I picked up the light metal strip to run my thumb up and down its textured sides. Did it help me to focus and to channel restless energy instead of twisting my hair? I think it did. Though research is in the early stages, many people, including people with autism spectrum disorder or attention-deficit/hyperactivity disorder, find that sensory fidget toys are helpful.

These days, in moments of anxiety or tension, many people reach for their smartphones. While some people want to spend less time on their phones, for others these devices can be a real help. A friend told me, "If we'd had smartphones when I was a teenager, I never would have started smoking. When I felt awkward, I'd light a cigarette just to give myself something to do. Now I'd be able to pull out my phone."

Touch can be a source of comfort, and it can also be a source of delight, so I looked for opportunities to upgrade my texture environment. One afternoon, in a fit of clutter-clearing energy, I was examining the contents of my closet to identify any rarely worn items to donate. I realized that although I liked the look of my three cotton shirts, I almost never wore them. Why not? I didn't like the texture of the stiff, smooth cotton. In the future, I'd pay as much attention to how an item felt against my skin as to how it looked to my eyes.

I like silkiness, and the next time I talked to Elizabeth, I said, "Your Blankey has satin edges. Did you love that material?"

"It's so old now, the satin border is totally gone," she said. "But I love anything silky. When I was little, I remember, I asked for a silk pillowcase for my birthday." I made a mental note to buy her a silk pillowcase.

On the other hand, some people dislike that silky, slick feeling. A friend and I were talking about how much we loved plushy textures—"A robe has to be plushy. A thin cotton robe shouldn't even count as a robe," he told me—but he added, "I hate anything silky or satiny. It makes my skin crawl."

I noticed for the first time how much I love velvet. In fact, my favorite room in our apartment features several velvety fabrics: two pillows of green velvet, two chairs covered in chenille, and a sofa covered in velvety corduroy.

One day at the drugstore, I walked past a display of Lava soap. As a railroad engineer, my grandfather came home with oily grime on his hands, so he used a gritty pumice soap. I bought a bar of Lava, took it home, and unwrapped it. Its soapy, sandy texture carried me right back to childhood.

The more I explored my sense of touch, the more I realized how much I valued it. How had touch faded into the background for me when it gave me such pleasure? I didn't know. But now that I'd started to pay attention, I found so much to delight me, right at my fingertips.

At some friends' dinner party, I found myself standing transfixed in front of a tabletop arrangement of pink peonies. Their glowing color and faint fragrance gave me a shock of joy, and I couldn't resist touching the soft, dewy petals. I heard a voice from behind me say, "Oh, aren't those flowers beautiful," in a pointed tone, and I snatched back my hand, feeling guilty.

As a child, I'd been told, "Don't touch," and now I was touching more than ever. How I loved the world! I didn't want to let it slide through my fingers, lost and forgotten.

Drenching My Sense of Touch

The autumn season made me think of the harvest, even though the only sign of any actual harvest in my neighborhood was outside the corner grocery store, where a soggy hay bale slumped beneath a pile of pumpkins and threw its musty scent into the air. Every time I walked past, I couldn't resist reaching out to rub my hand across the cool, smooth rind of a pumpkin.

Through my investigations, I'd learned that I could experience a sensation more deeply by switching it off and on. So, to explore my sense of touch, I decided to try a sensory deprivation tank (though apparently the term *sensory deprivation* has been replaced by *sensory enhancement*—very on-trend). I located a "floatation therapy center" whose website explained that by floating in complete silence and darkness, without the influence of gravity or tactile sensations, visitors would enter a state of deep relaxation. The center was just twenty minutes from my apartment, so I booked an appointment.

When the day came, as I buzzed up from the street, I wondered if the place would be deserted—who visited a sensory enhancement tank at 11:00 on a Wednesday morning? But there was a quiet bustle about the place. It looked like any day spa, with lots of natural light, plants, quiet music, and rows of items for sale.

An attendant led me back to a shower room and showed me the "floatation cabin." I'd pictured myself lying in a closed, confining pod, so I was relieved to see that the cabin was the size of a roomy walk-in closet, with a high ceiling, and filled wall to wall with ten inches of warm water.

Once I was alone, I took off my clothes, opened the tank's door, and gingerly stepped down several inches into the little room full of water—which, I'd read, was set to a skin-receptor-neutral 93.5 degrees Fahrenheit and saturated with Epsom salts to allow effortless floating. I slowly lay back to flatten myself across the water.

Once I'd shut the door and was settled in the darkness, I could feel my heart beat, and my breathing sounded very loud. But while I was more aware of my own body, I didn't experience the sense of "dissolution" or "deep relaxation" that I'd hoped for. My neck started to ache, my wax earplugs leaked, and I could sense the footsteps of people walking in the hallway. When it was time to stand up and open the door, I was happy to go.

Afterward, when I told a friend that I hadn't benefited from the sensory deprivation—ahem, enhancement—experience, he said, "Oh, I did that, too, and I kept thinking, 'When am I going to experience the magic?' It was so boring, I got out ten minutes early." It was good to hear that I wasn't the only one who found the experience disappointing.

Taking this sensory deprivation bath got me thinking about ordinary baths. My father-in-law is a huge fan.

"What do you like so much about baths?" I asked him.

"I like getting all that hot water around me."

"Is it because of your bad back?"

"No, I just like a bath."

"Do you take one every day?"

"Every day, and sometimes twice a day."

"*Twice?*"

"Yes. In the morning, and after I do the exercise bike." (He was quite amused by my curiosity about his attitude toward baths.)

On the other hand, a friend told me he hated the feeling of being immersed in water; he made his showers as brief as possible and never took a bath, never went into the ocean, and never jumped into a swimming pool. We all bring our own preferences to the possibilities of sensations.

After my touch-based adventure in the tank, I decided to bring the exercise back home, with a basic shower. Research shows that a shower or bath can help us wake up *or* fall asleep, boost our spirits, and give us a chance to step away from other people, our devices, and the tasks vying for our attention. Because we're both alert and relaxed, and beyond the reach of distractions, it's often a time when people have fresh ideas.

When one sense shuts down, the others become more acute, so one morning I started the water, then flipped off the light switch. The bathroom had no windows, so I stood in complete darkness.

I groped my way into the shower and was astonished by how much more intensely I felt the experience: the sensation of the warm water rushing over my body, the echo of water hitting the tiles, the soap's sandalwood smell, and the satisfying feeling of shampoo lathering in my hands. As Helen Keller observed, "Touch has its ecstasies."

Sensory enhancement achieved.

Touching the Intangible

As humans, we spend a significant amount of time thinking about abstract ideas, but nevertheless—or probably for this very reason— we find it deeply satisfying to handle actual objects.

With their solid presence, physical objects remind us of the people, places, and activities that we love. When something is important to me, I want to embody it in something that I can see and, just as important, touch.

Transcendent ideas and emotions gain power when they take physical form. When abstractions are made concrete through objects, art, or metaphor, they're easier to grasp—because they're easier to grasp. Physical objects can help us visualize the unobservable and touch the intangible, whether we're saluting a flag, putting on a judge's robes, or wearing the jersey of a favorite football team.

My visits to the Met showed me the importance of tangible objects in religious and cultural traditions to embody—and if possible, invoke—blessings such as "salvation," "justice," "good fortune," "victory," and "health," and even specific goods like "watchtower," "cattle," and "accountants."

People love to touch the sacred; making contact with something divine brings a blessing. According to "contagious magic," when we touch items that carry spiritual power, we acquire their protection. At the Met, many of my favorite objects were reliquaries that held some artifact of a saint, like the serene, somber *Enthroned Virgin and Child* or the covered bowl that held relics of the Buddha and small offerings.

More whimsically, for luck, people like to touch a statue, such as John Harvard's left foot in Cambridge or the snout of the Boar of Florence. (Note to the Met: Consider installing a statue that visitors could touch for luck. People would love it.)

Physical objects make transcendent values tangible, and so do physical rituals. After Christmas dinner every year, my mother passes a pack of "flying wish papers." We each take a sheet of tissue paper and write on it our secret wish for the new year. One by one, we roll our paper into a tube, stand it up straight, and light the tube with a match. If the tissue tube is rolled correctly, it quickly burns down, and its ash shoots high into the air—then we all cheer, and the wish will come true.

Gathering around a table, writing a secret wish, setting fire to the paper, the uncertainty of whether the ash will rise, the illusion of control—all these elements elevate our tradition. We have something to do and something to *touch* related to our hopes for the upcoming year.

Eliza told me that making this wish was one of her favorite holiday traditions. When I asked why, she explained, "It's unusual. Plus it combines the fun of a science-type experiment with making luck. I like doing something lucky or that makes my wish come true."

"Like blowing out candles on a birthday cake?"

"Right. Or finding a four-leaf clover, or throwing a coin into a fountain."

The next day at the Met, I threw a penny into the fountain in the Roman Sculpture Court. My lucky penny lay beside hundreds of the other coins, but only one coin was *mine*.

Superstition helps us believe that we have the power to influence events. Although most of us may not consider ourselves superstitious, we're a *littlestitious*. My father went to fly-fishing school, and on the last day, the instructor passed around a black velvet bag holding smooth river stones. "For fishing, you need technical skills, but you also need luck," he explained. "Reach into the bag, and your hand will be guided to the stone meant for you. Hold it, keep it in your fishing vest for luck."

I already had my lucky Hay scent, but studying the power of touching an object inspired me to identify an object that, as a family, we could all touch for luck.

A little store near my apartment sold natural curiosities, and there I found the perfect object: a small, polished cube of brilliant blue lapis lazuli streaked with pyrite. When I picked it up, I discovered that there was something disproportionately satisfying about its smooth, simple lines and deep color; it felt *just right* in the way few things do.

I brought it home and made an announcement to my family.

"I bought us this stone cube, for luck," I said. "I'm going to put it here on the bookshelf by the front door."

Eleanor reached out to take it from me. "It feels nice," she said as she passed it back and forth between her hands. "It's heavy."

"Whenever you need a little luck, touch the cube."

Although I'd expected them to be a little skeptical about my suggestion, they took it in stride. A few days later, as Eleanor got ready for school, I reminded her, "Don't forget to touch the cube on your way out the door. You've got your big test today!" She rolled her eyes, but she did it.

Using My Hands to Ignite My Imagination

Just as a touch can help us to engage with transcendent ideals, it can also help us to understand complex concepts.

The theory of "embodied cognition" holds that the body's experience shapes the way the mind thinks, and research shows that working with physical objects boosts our memory and helps us solve abstract problems. A teacher can point to a plastic model to show students the structure of a double helix; an ophthalmologist can use a model of an eye to help a patient understand a diagnosis.

For some time, I'd been working on something that seemed quite unrelated to the subject of embodied cognition. As one of my playing-hooky projects, I'd been making a list of "indirect directions" to help me generate creative solutions.

I started this list because I'd noticed a pattern in my writing life.

Sometimes, when working on a project, I'd hit a roadblock. Then, as I was struggling to move forward, I'd hear an offhand comment, or I'd read some thought-provoking phrase, and with this "indirect direction," I'd get sudden inspiration.

For instance, when working on my biography *Forty Ways to Look at Winston Churchill*, I was burdened by the sheer mass of information. I wanted to write a short, readable biography of Churchill that would nevertheless convey the tremendous scope of his life. How could I capture the complexity, the ambiguity, the humor, the tragedy—not to mention the extraordinary number of facts? It seemed impossible.

Then a friend mentioned that when she was writing her PhD dissertation, she kept a sticky note on her laptop that said, "Down with boredom." Whenever she felt bored by some part of her dissertation, she'd find a way to skip that material. This was a revelation to me: *I could skip the boring parts!* This "indirect direction" inspired the structure for my biography: I would skip the boring parts to focus only on the engaging aspects of Churchill's life.

Because this kind of random direction could be so illuminating, I kept a document that listed every "indirect direction" I found. Some were classic suggestions, such as "Embrace a constraint" and "Lower the bar." Some came from great artists, such as "The hardest thing in the world is simplicity" from writer James Baldwin and "Fill a box with items and images that inspire you" from choreographer Twyla Tharp. Others emerged from my own experience: "Collaborate with someone new," "Have something to say," "It's not a bug, it's a feature." (Of course, all directions won't work for all people. "Start a romance" is a proven approach—consider Picasso—but not a good idea for me.)

I collected these indirect directions, and when I felt stuck, I reviewed my list, and they often helped. For instance, the direction "Rearrange the pieces" solved a frustrating problem, and "Add ketchup" reminded me to include enough relish. As a digital document, however, this list on my computer felt insubstantial—plus I worried that I'd delete it or, more likely, at some point simply forget that I'd ever created it. I wanted to make it *real*.

As more experiences become virtual, the physical world becomes more exciting. Sometimes we put up with less convenience and more expense in order to use a satisfying physical tool; we'd rather have something less handy but in our hands. A friend paid extra to the phone company to activate his old-fashioned rotary desk phone. Eliza and Eleanor both traded small, light earbuds for big over-ear headphones. It took me years to give up my beloved Filofax; a digital calendar was far more practical but not nearly as satisfying.

I couldn't figure out what to do with my indirect-directions document, until one afternoon, when I was visiting my parents, I discovered my father's ancient Rolodex on a high closet shelf. I lifted it down with delight—I loved its heft, the old-fashioned look of the typed contact information, the way the faded cards flipped smoothly under my hand. Even though it was no longer useful, it was so *pleasing*.

Then it hit me: I'd use a Rolodex for my indirect directions! Actual physical cards would hold far more power than the ghostly list stored on my laptop. Filling out the cards would force me to refine my list, choosing a card at random would inspire unpredictable creative sparks, and holding a physical card would make a deeper impression in my mind.

I bought myself a rotary Rolodex, found my favorite set of colored markers, and copied each indirect direction onto a card. It was deeply satisfying to see the ideas presented in this physical form—and the ideas themselves seemed more powerful.

In fact, as soon as I'd finished copying my indirect directions, I realized that I already needed to use my Rolodex. What should I call this creation? I'd been using the phrase "Indirect Directions," but I wanted something better. "Rolodex of Ideas"? Nope.

I set the Rolodex in front of me and silently stated my creative challenge: "What's a good name for this tool?" Then I spun the knob, pulled out a card at random, and read, "Find a fresh metaphor."

I considered metaphors for a few minutes, but nothing occurred to me, so I stuck the card on my bulletin board. I hadn't solved my problem, but I did feel like the universe was telling me something and that I'd taken a constructive step toward a solution.

Would this process have been so satisfying if I'd clicked a box on a website to generate a prompt or opened a digital file to read it? No. The sense of agency I got from making a choice, reading the direction, and posting the card next to my desk . . . these physical actions made me feel in control, yet also directed by fate. We all want to cast our own dice. What's more, the sight of the physical card on my corkboard gave weight to its instruction and reminded me to think about it.

I kept the Rolodex on my desk and, from time to time, flipped through the cards: Top of desk equaled "top of mind." Along the same lines, a friend kept his recipe box out on the kitchen counter to inspire him to cook; another kept a set of note cards on her desk, so that at odd moments she was prompted to dash off a note to a friend. An acquaintance told me how she'd switched from physical photographs to digital photographs, and then switched back. "For me," she said, "digital photos didn't seem *real*. I had too many, I never looked at them, I worried about them vanishing in the ether. I want actual photos to hold." Some tasks are suited to the virtual world; for others, the physical is better.

As I walked through the Met one afternoon, I stopped in front of one of my favorite objects, the elaborate maiolica *Inkstand with Apollo and the Muses,* a desk set from 1584 decorated with figures of Apollo, the Muses, and famous poets. As I looked, I thought, "An inkstand with a crowd of muses is the perfect thing to spark ideas for a writer," and suddenly I knew what I should name my indirect-directions cards: the *Muse Machine*.

I laughed out loud at the pleasure of hitting upon this metaphor.

Making the Daily Visit

As I'd seen with the *Inkstand with Apollo and the Muses,* the Met's galleries were packed with examples of the human impulse to embody transcendent ideals and emotions in tangible objects, and its collection demonstrated our love for things we can hold.

If I wanted to use my own sense of touch at the Met, I could head to the gift shop. There, I'd be allowed to take artworks into my own hands—in the form of jewelry, tote bags, books, housewares, toys, and stationery—and I could even bring them home.

Museum gift shops are always better than regular gift shops, but as much as I love a museum gift shop, this area—like a café—can seem like an afterthought, almost disreputable. When he died in 1980, artist Clyfford Still left a huge trove of his work to whatever American city would build and dedicate a museum to him alone— but, he stipulated, the museum couldn't have a café or gift shop. It was thirty-one years before a museum opened.

Maybe the popularity of a gift shop means that, in the end, we're all just greedy consumerists. Does a salad plate printed with *A Bouquet of Flowers* trivialize that masterpiece? Does a figure of Frida Kahlo as a knitted key chain insult the artist's dignity?

I don't think so.

Material desires have a spiritual aspect, and the gift shop is an expression of the human wish to touch, to buy, to remember. When we see something we admire, we want to keep it, take a photo of it, break off a piece of it, or show it to others. It's easy to be sniffy about refrigerator magnets, but every pilgrim wants to bring home a scallop shell.

The gift-shop version may be a flimsy replica, but it's also how we hold a work of art in our own hands. Owning something, or its reproduction, changes our relationship to it. My grandmother had a framed print of Monet's *The Houses of Parliament, Sunset,* hanging above her living-room sofa in Nebraska. Seeing the print over and over, in her little house, made a different impression on me than the original did, when I eventually encountered it in the National Gallery in Washington, D.C.—and my familiarity with her copy made me see the original in a different way, too.

Walking past the gift shop's racks of items gave me an idea for a new exercise in attention. I bought postcards of several of my favorite works, then walked around the museum to compare the card to the original.

I saw that in person, the *Queen Mother Pendant Mask: Iyoba* from the Court of Benin is carved from ivory that glows in subtle shades, but the postcard flattens its color and textures. On the other hand, holding the postcard upside down and sideways in my hand helped me to appreciate the piece's elegant symmetries.

I'd gazed at Bruegel the Elder's *The Harvesters* many times, and I'd never quite registered the landscape in the distance, where buildings lined the seashore—but on the postcard, that element stood out. Holding the postcard in my hand, instead of looking at the painting on the wall, helped me understand its composition.

Going to the *Immersive Van Gogh* exhibit had given me a fresh perspective on *Self-Portrait with a Straw Hat*. Being able to move the postcard from up close to my eyes to farther away, next to the painting, helped me notice the way the brushstrokes on Van Gogh's hat and skin resembled the petals of his sunflowers in other paintings.

After these postcard exercises, any time I walked past these artworks, they seemed to jump out at me. They felt more *mine* because I'd held them in my hand, even in that artificial, miniature way.

A purchase is also a way to prove that "I was there, I saw it myself, I took something away"—though these days, many people skip buying the calendar and take a selfie with an artwork instead. I felt the urge to buy something myself, and in the gift shop I bought a miniature copy of "William." This bright blue hippo stat-

uette from ancient Egypt has become the Met's mascot, and he appears on everything from tote bags to toys.

This little hippo was a physical representation of my love of my daily visits—and gave me a way to hold my own piece of the Met.

Touching More

More and more, I noticed how my five-senses investigations had deepened my experience of everyday life. The world seemed more magnificent and compelling—and it also felt more comfortable and convenient.

For instance, when I started paying attention, I felt sheepish about the helpful touch-cues that I'd never noticed. As I'd learned in my high school typing class, when typing, I always returned my two index fingers to the *F* and *J* keys. Now I realized that my keyboard had little raised bumps on *F* and *J*, so I could make sure my hands were aligned properly without looking. My recording headphones had a small bump on the headband on the left side, so I didn't have to search for the inconspicuous *L* to put them on correctly.

With my sense of touch, I'd found a helpful source of calm and focus. When I was feeling anxious or annoyed, holding my little William statuette helped restore me to my Met mindset—calm, curious, unhurried, and expansive. I developed the habit of holding the figurine in my hand as a physical reminder to take the long view.

I'd often read advice such as "Hold an object and focus your attention on its texture, weight, and color." Now I found that just holding the cool, rounded figure helped to anchor me in the moment. I didn't pay attention to how it looked; its mere heft helped steady my thoughts.

Also, my sense of touch could give me so much pleasure. During a work trip, I stayed at a hotel with a heated bathroom floor. I'd read about this luxury feature but never experienced it before—and as someone who's always cold, I loved it. I kept returning to the bathroom to lie across the tiles. Back home, looking through my closet, I realized that even though my favorite sweatshirt was looking worn, I didn't want to get rid of it—it was the perfect mix of warm, soft, and stretchy.

Along with sheer enjoyment, touch offered the superpower of playfulness. I bought a box of kinetic sand to explore its weird properties and used my favorite markers in a coloring book. Research shows that we get a real boost from play, with improved brain function, increased ability to generate ideas, and a better sense of humor and perspective. I wasn't a particularly lighthearted person—I tended more toward the brisk and practical—and my sense of touch helped me to amplify the playful element of my nature.

More playfulness meant more creativity. During a shower one morning, as I was making shapes from the soapy lather on my hands, I was suddenly struck by a realization.

Out of nowhere, I thought, "The Met includes a great example of the Muse Machine direction 'Incorporate something whole from somewhere else.'" I pictured the sunny European Sculpture Court. Years ago, when the Met expanded, its south exterior was swallowed by its newer, larger building. Now the former entrance stands complete but tucked inside, as one wall of a sculpture court.

I felt such intense pleasure at making this connection that I thought, "I should write a Muse Machine handbook where I discuss each direction and give examples." *Yes!* As soon as I'd jumped out of the shower, I scribbled a note to myself (another Muse Machine direction is "Make note of every idea; don't trust your memory"), and I felt the excitement that I always get when I begin a new project. And before I typed my first word of this handbook, I vowed, I would hold my blue cube—for luck.

Nevertheless, the most important superpower of touch was to

make me feel closer to other people. I appreciated, as never before, how much comfort I got from physical touch.

When we were walking together, Jamie often put his arm around my shoulder or reached for my hand. I no longer took this habit for granted; now I realized how happy it made me. Far more often, I was reaching for his hand.

As I went through my days, I thought of the past, present, and future; I daydreamed; I planned; I ruminated and forgot. Jamie's touch reminded me to reach out for the person I loved who was right here, right now.

Onward

◎ 〰 ⓒ ♥ ⓐ

The Chief Inlets of Soul, or How the Body Can Minister to the Spirit (and Vice Versa)

Man has no Body distinct from his Soul. For that called Body is a portion of Soul discerned by the five senses, the chief inlets of Soul in this age.
—WILLIAM BLAKE, *The Marriage of Heaven and Hell*

ONE RECENT NIGHT, AS WE SAT WITH FRIENDS AROUND A RES-
taurant's crowded table, I took a moment to reflect on why I
was having such a good time.

Most important, I was spending the evening with people I loved.
We sat together with no distractions or interruptions to detract from
our pleasure of one another's company.

The room's heavy curtains and plush cushions gave it an intimate, cozy atmosphere, and the sounds of other people's conversations gave the room a feeling of energy without making it hard to
hear. I admired one friend's heavy, old-fashioned wristwatch and
another's delicate gold necklace. I caught the light fragrance of
flowers in a vase near our table, and from time to time, I picked up

Jamie's glass of scotch to take a big sniff (I don't like the taste of scotch, but I enjoy the smell of it). I ordered salmon and noted its rich flavor and warmth as I took my first bite. I appreciated the cool weight of the cutlery and the soft, worn velvet that covered my chair.

Before I'd started my five-senses investigation, I would've enjoyed myself, but in a general way, with no understanding of how these elements came together to make this evening particularly pleasant. Because I noticed more, I appreciated more.

GENERALLY, IN MY WORK, I reflect on the large subject of happiness: How can we make ourselves happier, healthier, more productive, and more creative? How can we change, if we want to change? How can we know ourselves more deeply?

Again and again, these questions return me to the principles of *self-knowledge* and *mindful action*. I use self-knowledge to guide my mindful action toward a happier life.

At the start of this project, I'd seen the lurid pink of my eyes and been jolted into a new respect for my five senses, and since that day, I'd tried countless five-senses experiments. I talked to a ballet dancer about the power of feeling the floor and the hazards of lifting a dancer wearing a tutu; I wore a nasal strip to see if it would change my taste perception; I tried the popular 5-4-3-2-1 grounding exercise; I tried cryotherapy; I toured the casinos of Las Vegas; I surprised Eleanor with a pan of Jiffy Pop.

Most adventurous: I'd tried ayahuasca. My study of the senses had made me curious to try the heightened perceptions of a psychedelic experience. (Because new research suggested that psychedelics could be a useful therapeutic tool, this kind of experiment seemed more promising and less scary.) I got in touch with a researcher, made a plan, and steeled myself for the unknown. After I drank a thick, gritty, bitter tea, I threw up three times—then, after some visual effects that reminded me of an overly bright department store, I fell asleep, and woke up feeling normal. I hadn't experienced the intense sensations I'd hoped for, but I did feel exhilarated by the experiment. I'd done something out of the ordinary, something that intimidated me.

These experiences showed me that I, like everyone, lived in my own world of sensations, created from my own body, experiences, culture, and idiosyncrasies; what's more, with mindful action, I could shape my experience through my senses. I possessed the senses' superpowers!—if I made the effort to use them.

It was a constant challenge to *notice*. In artist Scott Polach's *Applause Encouraged #111415*, guests watched the sun set over the ocean, then applauded. In my own life, how could I maintain the discipline of noticing? A friend once told me, "After my trip to India, I had no doubt that I was going to cook with cumin all the time. But I don't." I knew exactly what he meant. It was easier to *feel* transformed than to *be* transformed. I wanted to maintain my focus on my five senses as I moved onward into the future.

Before I started my investigation, though I hadn't realized it, I'd been doing a lot of looking and not enough listening; now I was tuning in to each of my five senses. I also learned how much power I had to design my environment. To add pleasure, I could wear perfume to bed, visit a museum every day, and pet Barnaby's silky ears. When I walked closer to a jasmine vine, the fragrance gave me a hit of pleasure so intense that it seemed to lift me off the ground. To reduce annoyances, I could turn off my phone notifications, give away a scratchy pair of pants, or fix a wobbly chair. Instead of reusing that smelly, worn kitchen sponge one more time, I could replace it with a new one.

In fact, even though I was celebrating my senses as never before, I kept dreaming up new ways to explore them. I knew that by going through my body, I could reach my spirit, and through my spirit, I could reach my body.

More Delight

When I started my experiment, I hoped that my five senses would help me find more delight—an aim that, for me, was neither easy nor obvious. Writer Samuel Butler observed, "There is no greater sign of a fool than the thinking that he can tell at once and easily what it is that pleases him." Or in the immortal words of the Cat in the Hat:

> *Look at me!*
> *Look at me!*
> *Look at me NOW!*
> *It is fun to have fun*
> *But you have to know how.*

That had been my question: *How?* I'd learned that I could turn to my five senses.

When I was feeling anxious, annoyed, frustrated, or bored, I could wear a bright color, listen to a favorite song, taste an old family recipe, or give a hug. The power of my attention elevated even the most ordinary moments—of walking Barnaby, making the bed, looking at my old "3D Magic Eye" autostereogram postcards. When I walked through a toy store, I took a moment to flip the reversible sequins on a pillow, to feel the disks slide under my fingers as their color shifted from gold to silver. I'll never forget the thrill of seeing the brilliantly scarlet leaves of a Japanese maple tree glowing against a dark sky.

Whenever someone pointed out a particularly enjoyable sensation, their appreciation helped me to enjoy it more myself. I noticed the color "Ultra Violet" after Pantone named it the "Color of the Year," and I remembered how much I loved the song "Scarborough Fair" after I heard it on the soundtrack of the movie *The Graduate*. When I took the time to read a menu's elaborate description of the chicken dish, I could pick up the flavor of ginger. After my mother remarked, "I love walking down the street and seeing the flowers for sale outside the little delis," I began to take pleasure in those flowers as well.

One popular way to observe the world more closely is to take a daily photo, the way a friend takes a photo of the Hudson River every morning. While many people argue that taking photos can diminish our enjoyment, some research suggests that taking photos actually helps us engage more deeply.

The photo-taking approach didn't appeal to me; I always turn to words. To help myself taste the guacamole and feel the sheepskin, I decided to start a Five-Senses Journal.

I pulled a lined notebook from a shelf and wrote "See," "Hear," "Smell," "Taste," and "Touch" down the page. At the end of every day, I would note my most memorable sensations.

My first day's entries of sense-highlights included:

See: gorgeous silvery black fur of a Weimaraner dog, looked
    frosted
Hear: walking downtown, heard church bells chime the hour
Smell: Barnaby needs a bath
Taste: surprising, delicious smoky flavor in a salad
Touch: scratchy sisal rug in Judy and Bob's apartment

My Five-Senses Journal proved to be invaluable as a quick daily reminder to maintain my focus on my five senses forever—and it also felt like a gratitude journal. How many moments passed through me, intense, endless, but unremembered? I must notice, I must appreciate.

I perceived more beauty, and—I had to admit—more stink, mess, and racket. Once I heard how much noise a refrigerator could make, I couldn't un-hear it. Once I registered the sourness of coffee, I tasted it far more often. But I was willing to pay the price of perception, because feeling the full range of sensation made me feel more present, more alive. It gave me the sense of *vitality* that I craved.

In my ordinary life, my desire to be productive could make it hard to stray from my to-do list. Because of my five senses, I had more fun. One afternoon, Eleanor and I made a non-Newtonian fluid with cornstarch—liquid and solid at the same time, like quicksand—and laughed as we squeezed it, tapped it, and dragged our fingers through it. My search for scarlet gave me an excuse to visit B&J Florist Supply, and I felt the thrill of the hunt every time I spotted my color among their fake foods and flowers.

I also started to play five-senses pranks on my family. Eleanor was mystified after I snuck some "Gelling Joke" into her coffee to turn it into nontoxic, nonedible sludge, and I used trick relighting candles for Jamie's birthday cake.

One day, when my family and I were all weary of the frigid December weather, I had an inspiration: We'd head to the Bronx to visit the New York Botanical Garden. I rallied everyone to go, and as we walked through the park entrance toward the glass-domed conservatory, the grounds looked drab, limp, and brown.

Inside the magnificent greenhouse, though, the plants were bursting with life and color. My favorite exhibit was the *Lowland Tropical Rain Forest,* where lush greenery crowded every surface and branches met above our heads, in growth so dense that it muffled sound.

"I love it when the outdoors comes indoors," I told Eliza.

"Me too," she answered. She slid her coat off her shoulders, and I pulled off my hat, as we all slowly made our way down the path. I could feel the damp air pressing against my cheek.

"Smell it!" Eleanor said, as she gave a deep sniff. The heavy atmosphere held the rich, living scent of dirt and water, as well as the mixed green smells of unfamiliar vegetation. The contrast between this warm, vibrant interior and the cold, withered landscape outside gave the room a joyful quality.

We hadn't visited the New York Botanical Garden for ten years; as we walked back outside to return to the park's front gate, I heard Eleanor say to Eliza, "We should come back here when it's warm—maybe you're allowed to bring a picnic."

More Love

The more I learned about my five senses, the more I wanted to discuss them with other people. I kept saying things like "The smell of charcoal always makes me think of summer. How about you?" and "Did you know that elephants can hear the movement of clouds?" It turns out that talking about sensory experiences is a great way to connect with other people because it's a subject that interests just about everyone.

In particular, my five senses also helped me grow closer to the people I loved by helping me observe the details of their actual presence—so beloved but so easy to take for granted.

I realized that just as I could use my five senses to know *myself* better, I could use them to know *someone else* better. To help myself look more closely at Jamie, I created a Five-Senses Portrait of him. I grabbed a notebook and wrote JAMIE at the top of the page.

When I thought of Jamie . . .

I thought of seeing . . .
1. *The way he folded back newspapers as he read them*
2. *Our coat closet full of his jackets*
3. *Him stretched out on the sofa for a Sunday nap*
4. *The striking colors of the rose-red fleece jacket and chartreuse knit shirt that he often wore in the early days of our relationship*
5. *His red, sweaty face after he finished exercising*

I thought of hearing . . .

1. His voice saying, "Let's gaze lovingly" before cracking open the door so we could peek at Eliza, then Eleanor, asleep in a crib
2. The congratulatory music that played every time he finished a New York Times crossword puzzle on his iPad
3. Sports talk on his favorite podcast
4. His voice talking in business terms
5. His long, slow breaths when he was in a very deep sleep

I thought of smelling . . .

1. The whisky he liked to drink in the evening
2. His tennis bag
3. The outdoors, brought in every night after he took Barnaby for a nighttime walk
4. Laundry detergent that floated out every time he pulled a cotton T-shirt over his head
5. Gillette shaving cream

I thought of tasting . . .

1. The Life Savers he often ate
2. Ice cream—once a week, Jamie celebrated "Ice Cream Saturday"
3. Mint toothpaste, when I gave him a good-morning kiss
4. The peanut butter he spooned out from the jar as an after-dinner snack
5. Coffee with milk, the way he drank it

I thought of touching . . .

1. The springy hair on the top of his head
2. The skin on the top of his leg, which was hairless, because that's where he gave himself injections when he was in a trial to cure his hepatitis C (now cured)
3. The sharp, rough ends of the plastic straws that he chewed and left around the apartment

4. *His warm bare shoulder against my cheek*
5. *The sticky keys of our family laptop, because he ate while he used it*

Doing this Five-Senses Portrait helped me appreciate Jamie's physical presence in a way that I hadn't done in a long time—and noticing the *outer* Jamie gave me an insight into the *inner* Jamie. For instance, I saw that he'd bought himself a few button-down shirts in a new style—more fitted, with more pattern. These changes were subtle, but I noticed and realized, "Jamie's feeling ready to shake things up."

As I was telling a friend about this exercise, she pulled out her phone. "I'm sending myself an email. I want to remember this idea," she said as she typed. "My grandfather died a few months ago, and this would be a great way to hold on to my memories."

As I tuned in to my five senses, I became much more aware of the people around me. I noticed how my father's posture improved after he started targeting different muscles during his workouts, how Eliza started wearing hair clips, and how a friend started using words like *deliverables, stakeholders,* and *bandwidth* after she took a new job. Picking up on these little details made me feel more attuned to the people who were important to me.

And just as the five senses helped me to *notice* other people, they also provided a great bridge to *connect* with other people. We often enjoy a sense-experience more when we share it. *Saturday Night Live* seemed funnier when people across the country were also watching; the Met's Chinese Garden Court looked more beautiful when I was showing it to a friend who was astonished to find an actual garden—complete with fresh, bright plants and a koi pond—deep inside the museum's second floor.

When an old friend was going through an exceptionally rough time, I decided to send her a sense-experience in the mail. Just as we can minister to the body through the spirit, sometimes we can minister to the spirit through the body, and while bodily pleasures may be fleeting, they do bring their own energy and comfort. I assembled a sensorium gift to please or ease each of her five senses:

- Sight: a set of beautiful colored pencils
- Sound: a tiny hand-cranked music box that played the song "You Are My Sunshine"
- Smell: a box of three small candles, each with a different scent
- Taste: a sampler of salts
- Touch: a soft, light throw blanket in a deep blue

The body can be a refuge, a calming distraction, and a source of vitality—plus we all love surprises and treats. Usually, I was stumped when I tried to think of a good gift, but thinking about the five senses made gift-giving easier and more fun. Whether the items were inexpensive, lavish, silly, or comforting, someone would love to unpack that box—I could even imagine a workplace sensorium box, to bring a team together.

A *thing* can also be an *experience,* and in physical form, we can make a gift of an experience, to embody our love so it can be seen, heard, smelled, tasted, or touched.

More Energy

One of my most unexpected discoveries was the way we can turn to our senses for energy and self-renewal. Taking care of our sensory environments can be an important (and cheap and easy) way to care for ourselves.

Instead of passively enduring the sensations around me, I could actively shape them. When I wanted an immediate jolt of energy and cheer, I could take a quick sniff of grapefruit, revel in the luxurious cushion of new cotton socks, or listen to a favorite song from my Audio

Apothecary. If I felt sluggish, I could take a quick walk outside, where I could gaze at the clouds, brush my hand against a lamppost's cold, bumpy surface, and sample whatever unpredictable smells would float by me on the street—and, with these sensations, wake myself up.

While it's wonderful to give ourselves a quick treat, we don't want to do something to make ourselves feel *better* that just makes us feel *worse*—such as binge-watching, doomscrolling, or eating too much Halloween candy. Scents and sounds, however, can be indulged with abandon. I can't glut myself on fragrance, and there's no downside to listening to more music (as long as the volume isn't turned up too high).

I also realized that all energy isn't the same. I wasn't looking for a restless, jittery energy that would leave me feeling unsettled and agitated; I wanted a calm energy that gave me focus and stamina.

In gambling, a "tell" is a change in behavior that reveals a person's inner state, and I'd noticed that I had a tell in everyday life: Whenever I felt anxious, I'd try to reduce my sensory load. I'd stop wearing perfume, or I'd ask Eleanor to turn down her music, because suddenly, that extra scent or sound felt overwhelming.

On the other hand, some people get relief from an intense hit of sensation, which can distract them from negative thoughts and return them to the physical world. They might plunge their hands or face into cold water, suck on an ice cube, take a hot shower, turn on loud music, or bite into a lemon.

Even before I knew this principle, I'd applied it with great success. When Eliza was in tenth grade, she fell into a terrible funk before exams, and she couldn't muster up the focus and energy to study. I couldn't figure out a way to help—until suddenly I had an inspiration.

"Come on," I told her as she sat staring into space above her textbook. "Get up. We're going!"

"Where?" she asked, startled.

"You've been begging to get a third piercing for your ear, and now we're going. Figure out a reputable place, and we'll leave in half an hour."

"*Now?*" she asked, incredulous.

"Yes, but you've got a lot of studying to do, so we need to move."

"Okay, I'll find a place!" she answered. She scrambled into action. Two hours later, she had a new piercing in her ear and was back at her books. The surprise and physical shock of getting her ear pierced broke through her exam stress and gave her the energy to study.

A friend told me that after her older daughter left for college, she and her younger daughter consoled themselves by making a trip to a flower market. "We bought bunches of flowers," she said. "We made arrangements all over the apartment, and all that color and fragrance cheered us up."

Not long after hearing this story, my email stopped working, and I was overwhelmed by that distinctive anxiety caused by tech problems. I did something I never do: I bought some flowers, pulled out a glass vase, arranged the flowers, and carried the vase to my office.

I'd never kept flowers in my office before, and I was astonished by how much pleasure and energy they gave me. Flowers! Poet May Sarton remarked, "If someone asked me what my idea of luxury is, I think my answer would be: flowers in the house all year round."

My five-senses experiment had helped me to appreciate, in a way that I never had before, the beauty of flowers. I thought of Eliza's soft voice saying, "My mommy is having a flower party," and I realized, yet again, that I could minister to my spirit through my body—in this case, with a pharmacy of flowers.

I made a note to add to my Muse Machine: *Fill every vase with flowers.*

More Imagination

When I began my five-senses investigation, I'd hoped that it might spark my creativity and productivity—and as it turned out, I was unprepared for just *how* sparked I'd get.

My visits to the Met, in particular, fired my imagination. These daily breaks reminded me of a time I'd almost forgotten: recess. As a child, I was good at sitting still, focusing on my work, and finishing my assignments. But I loved recess, too, when I was out of the classroom, on the playground, and doing whatever I felt like doing. It was daily but unstructured. It was creative and playful. I wasn't trying to achieve some practical purpose, like "improve my concentration," "lift my heart rate," or "direct my awareness," and I didn't have to follow instructions. I was enjoying each of my five senses.

As an adult, I was still good at sitting still, focusing on my work, and finishing my assignments—and with my visits to the Met, I'd given myself the freedom of recess. Other people might use meditation to help them train their thoughts; I used recess to help me liberate my thoughts.

After recess, it was easier to return to my desk. Research shows that breaks from mental effort help us stay productive and creative, and insights often emerge during times when our minds roam freely—before getting out of bed in the morning, during a commute, in the shower, during exercise. As writer Virginia Woolf observed, "My mind works in idleness. To do nothing is often my most profitable way."

Which means that play is not idleness.

Also, I realized that for many people, including me, tools and raw ingredients spark imagination. It's the limitless possibilities these materials represent, and it's also the sensory stimulation offered by bunches of fragrant herbs, baskets of soft yarn, or a guitar leaning against a wall, ready to play.

I was surprised to realize that these kinds of materials fired up my imagination, even when I had no intention of using them myself. Before I'd started my investigation, I wondered if my focus on the senses might inspire me to start a new sense-based activity like painting, making collages, or cooking, but that didn't happen. Instead, my five-senses experiment intensified my usual creative urge—to make things with *words*. I would look at rows of brilliantly colored paints and be inspired not to pick up a brush but to sit down at my computer. A friend had writer's block, and I told him, "Visit a hardware store, a farmers market, or a place that sells art supplies or musical instruments. If you're like me, it will give you ideas."

Tapping into my senses stimulated my writerly imagination in many directions. I kept tinkering with my playing-hooky book of "My Color Pilgrimage." I'd drawn up my Manifesto for Listening and my Tastes Timeline. I'd created a Five-Senses Journal. Every single day I worked on my favorite project, my "Book of Aphorisms." I'd created my Muse Machine—and I was also making notes for a handbook to accompany it. (I was astonished to realize how many Muse Machine ideas I'd used during the writing of this very book; among others, "Examine the same thing over and over," "Review old notes," "Big ending," "Expose the architecture of ideas—or hide it," and, of course, "Consult an oracle.")

Everything was interesting. *Everything* was beautiful. I could walk into any room and call it a museum. Psychiatrist and psychoanalyst Carl Jung noted, "The creative mind plays with the object it loves," and I'd learned how to play from the objects around me.

And the other day, I did something I'd never done before: I brought a sketchpad and pencil to the Met.

As I'd explored the sensory world, it had taken me a long time to grasp an essential paradox. On the one hand, we could spark our creativity by engaging our five senses in something new or interesting. Unusual, overwhelming experiences such as *Immersive Van Gogh* or a sound bath helped me generate ideas; so did flipping through my Muse Machine.

On the other hand, we could fire up our imaginations by putting ourselves in predictable, somewhat boring surroundings. To keep itself occupied during my familiar morning routine or visit to the Met, my mind would wander into unfamiliar insights. For instance, during what was probably my fiftieth visit to a particular room at the Met, I felt a bit bored—and then I experienced an electrifying flash of understanding.

A bunch of random facts and observations I'd made about the senses suddenly snapped together: *The beautiful often requires a bit of ugly.*

Based on what?

In 2012, to make mandatory cigarette packaging as unappealing as possible, researchers identified the most visually repellent color—Pantone 448 C, a cusp color of drab greenish-brown that has been compared, inelegantly, to "baby poop." After reading that it nevertheless appears in great artworks such as Leonardo da Vinci's *Mona Lisa,* I'd looked for this "ugly" color around the Met. Sure enough, I'd discovered, it added beauty to works such as Hendrick ter Brugghen's mournful *The Crucifixion with the Virgin and Saint John,* where it colors the dramatic night sky, and Camille Pissarro's peaceful landscape *Jalais Hill, Pontoise,* where it appears among the greens of fields and roofs.

During the Sondheim concert, I'd noted how often his music included surprising moments of dissonance, which, I'd later learned, many listeners in the Western tradition associate with clash and harshness. At the same time, dissonance can give music an unresolved quality that makes it more compelling—for instance, in the blues, in the music of the Romantic period, and in Sondheim.

My perfume professor had pointed out that to make a beautiful fragrance, it was sometimes necessary to add a touch of something bad-smelling. Such perfume-building ingredients have included civet paste (the secretion of a civet's perineal glands), hyraceum (petrified excreta of the rock hyrax), and ambergris (often referred to as "whale vomit," though it actually comes from the whale's other end).

In my study of taste, I'd learned that a hint of sour vinegar deepens the flavor of fruit preserves, a chocolate truffle rolled in bitter cocoa powder tastes better than a truffle rolled in confectioners' sugar, and a pinch of salt—unpleasant on its own—enhances every other flavor.

A dull moment during recess gave my imagination the opportunity to connect these unrelated facts. I had a new card to add to my Muse Machine creation: "Add a bit of ugly."

More Memories

Marcel Proust tasting his tea-soaked madeleine cookie is the most famous illustration of an intense, emotional memory sparked by the senses, but each of the five senses has the power to conjure up lost time. The sound of Jim Dale's voice reading from a Harry Potter book reminds me of my daughters' childhoods; the smell of hairspray reminds me of watching my mother and father get dressed for a party when I was a child.

Our five senses link us to our past, tie us to the present, and help us create memories for the future. They even help us conjure up memories that we've forgotten we possessed—and to recall a pleasure is to experience it twice. Plus, as I had learned with my mother-in-law, asking people about their sensory memories is a great way to get to know them better.

Because traditions repeatedly link vivid sensations to events, they create especially lasting memories. When I think back on Christmas with my family, I remember the glittering colors of the ornaments, the smell of evergreen branches and the piñon incense we burn only in December, the taste of the sausage soup that's our traditional Christmas Eve dinner, the feel of the woven yarn of the needlepoint stockings that our mother made for Elizabeth and me. These sensations—so specific, so familiar—help me hang on to my past.

Thinking about the relationship of the five senses to memory underscored an important truth for me: What's familiar is easy to ignore. The sights, sounds, smells, tastes, and textures of *today* are hard to notice because they're so familiar. It's so easy to forget that one day, *now* will be a long time ago.

For that reason, I decided to create an "Album of Now" to collect photos of my ordinary life. The days are long, but the years are short; at one point, I'd assumed I'd be singing "Good Morning to You" to a baby in a crib forever, and now I can hardly remember what that crib looked like—and I never bothered to take a photo of it. How many times had I opened my refrigerator? Its contents seem so dull, so unchanging—but my refrigerator held a very different set of items fifteen years ago. I could date my life by the changing designs on diet-soda cans.

I spent one Saturday photographing my everyday life: medicine cabinet, closets, shelves, rooms, and our building's lobby and elevator. I also took photos to remind me of sounds, smells, tastes, and textures—the electric waffle-maker in which I made my morning chaffle, Barnaby's favorite squeaky toy, my favorite hoodie.

I created a physical book from my photos, and when I sat leafing through its pages, these ordinary objects acquired new significance. Strangely, a copy of something real is often more compelling than the thing itself. By creating a snapshot of sensations, my Album of Now had given me a fresh way to notice my ordinary day.

This exercise made me want to look at more photos from unremarkable scenes from my past. But how?

Years ago, after my grandparents died, their house was sold—and it occurred to me that the house might have been listed on a real estate website. I typed in their street address and, sure enough, there it was. I could see the brick flower box where my grandmother grew purple and white petunias; the shaded back patio where my grandfather grilled hamburgers; the coarse, sanded paint on the walls of the room where Elizabeth and I slept. I even saw the small bathroom sink where my grandfather's Lava soap had sat on its special dish.

On my final visit to that house, on the white kitchen counter, very close to the edge, I had cut a narrow notch into the surface. I'd felt some kind of ancient impulse to make my mark on a beloved place that I would never visit again. I peered at the photo of the

kitchen to see if I could see it, and I imagined that, somehow, I could see that notch. These rooms were so ordinary; it was my memories and my love that made them remarkable.

A much-studied question in psychology is: "How much does a person's personality change over a lifetime?" And the unsatisfying answer is: "Somewhat, and it depends." As for me, I've always felt very much myself.

One of my earliest sensory memories was standing on a little step stool to wash my hands in the kindergarten bathroom. As I held my hands under the cool water, I looked at myself in the mirror and thought, "Here I am, this is *now*."

Do I remember that moment because it was then that I began to know, *I am*? I was both noticing my surroundings and catching myself in the very act of having a thought, the same kind of thought I still have—indeed, I'm having that very thought as I write this sentence. What I would give for a photograph of that room or a bottle that captured its kindergarten scent.

To be more present in the present, I had created my Album of Now—and of course, the minute I made the album, it became an artifact of the past. That's where the past begins: now.

Be Gretchen

Years ago, as an exercise in self-knowledge, I wrote a list of my Twelve Personal Commandments, the overarching principles by which I try to live my life. The first and most important is "Be Gretchen," and to do that, I must know myself. Self-knowledge is challenging, however, because it's so easy to be distracted by the way we wish we were, or what others think we should be, until we lose sight of what's actually true.

To be Gretchen, I must both *accept myself* and *expect more from myself*: strive to embrace the realities of my nature while also enlarging my sense of possibility. When I'd started my five-senses experiment, sight and smell were my foreground senses; hearing, taste, and (I'd wrongly assumed) touch were in the background.

My experiment had helped me to deepen pleasures from my foreground senses of sight and smell. I reveled in colors; I stopped to smell the flowers, literally. Even better, once I started attending to them, I got more pleasure from my neglected senses: I enjoyed music; I touched a card to unlock my imagination; I realized how much I loved the feel of velvet. True, I hadn't evolved into a more adventuresome eater, but I did have more appreciation for familiar tastes.

Also, my new awareness of my own unique sensory world reminded me that I may not have it forever. So often, we value what we have only once we've lost it or fear we might lose it. That conversation with my eye doctor had been brief, but it had been enough to remind me of the vulnerability of my five senses. And more than that—time itself would rob me of what I loved to see and touch, as everything around me sank into the past.

My senses were precious because of the sheer pleasure they gave me, but even more precious was their power to tie me to the people, places, and ordinary moments that I wanted to experience and remember from the drifting, ephemeral material of life.

OVER THE COURSE OF MY endeavors, more than anything else I did, visiting the Metropolitan Museum changed me.

By establishing my daily visit, I used my love of discipline to give myself a break from discipline (like passing through a gateless gate or phantom tollbooth). Recess gave me the chance to wander. In the past,

I'd always visited museums with other people; now museum-going seemed like a solo activity. Also, the prospect of visiting a museum or an exhibit a single time seemed almost . . . futile. What was the point of going just *once*? I may visit the Met every day for the rest of my life.

I'd chosen a museum, but, of course, someone else might choose a different place. A park, a route through a neighborhood, a front stoop—the place doesn't really matter. With familiarity and repetition, the world reveals itself in an unexpected way.

As for me, I chose the Met, and there I measured myself against a different scale. I felt myself rise above the trivialities of my daily life. As I read the placards' calm references to disaster—from the sack of Rome to the death of a beloved dog—my own worries receded. Works of coral, rock crystal, burr walnut, porcupine quills, gold leaf, clay, feathers, and jade transported me with their sublime transformations of nature.

Awe is an intensely gratifying emotion, and also research shows that people who experience awe more frequently show more humility and more creativity, have a greater sense of well-being and desire to connect with others, and even have better immune health. Awe decreases anxiety and stress.

But I didn't care about these utilitarian arguments; I visited the Met for pure joy. I felt happier from the moment I walked through its doors. It was a paradox: I felt more deeply inside myself, yet I also felt able to slide outside of myself and connect to the world. The Met became my playground, my tree house, my snow day.

I felt guilty about grubbing through the museum in my usual yoga pants and running shoes. In his student days, famous aesthete Oscar Wilde caused a national sensation when he remarked, "I find it harder and harder every day to live up to my blue china." I felt the same way. I stood in front of the stern, pure *God Horus Protecting King Nectanebo II* and thought, "How can I be worthy of it? How do I rise to the beauty of the world?" The best way was to reach out with my senses. No one else could visit my Metropolitan Museum.

There, nothing flashed, nothing spun; everything waited for me to come to it. As objects became more familiar, and as I learned more about them, they became more beautiful, so the Met slowly transformed itself beneath my gaze. Through my five senses, I'd inhabited the museum at last: I'd reached across it, plumbed it. And yet the Met was so huge, and reshaped itself so often, that it would never seem stale. When I returned for the tenth time to Borgianni's *Self Portrait as a Painter with Palette and Canvas,* I discovered that it had disappeared. I was happy that I'd looked carefully at the painting while I had the chance.

On one visit, as I walked through the Medieval Treasury gallery, I stopped, as I always did, to text a photo of the toothy cow to Eliza. For the first time, I noticed that in that stained glass window, a railing of pure scarlet ran behind the figures of Mary and Joseph, to set off their faces with brilliance. How had I never seen that before?

Then, as I was walking past a row of sunlit marble statues, I suddenly realized something obvious about my visits to the Metropolitan Museum: The Met was a *metaphor* for my entire undertaking.

When I started this project, I'd yearned to outgrow the accidental limitations of my nature, to experience more deeply this life, my only life. My visits were my attempt to reach the places in me that I hadn't yet discovered. Through my senses, I'd found my visible storage, my masterpieces set in illuminated cases, my neglected stairwells, my fountains, my postcards, my stone vases filled with flowers. I am the laboratory, I am the notebook, and I am the museum.

Epilogue

Wider Than the Sky

The Brain—is wider than the Sky—
For—put them side by side—
The one the other will contain
With ease—and you—beside—
                    —EMILY DICKINSON

BARNABY NEEDED HIS LATE-AFTERNOON WALK, SO WE HEADED outside. The weather report predicted rain, and I wanted to get back to my desk, so instead of letting him sniff and explore as usual, I hurried him along our route. As we paused on a corner for a red light, I happened to glance at an orange traffic cone sitting on the street near us.

This was a standard plastic cone, the kind I'd seen a thousand times and never really noticed. But at this moment, in the yellow-green light from the overcast sky, its orange shape glowed against the gray-blue of the asphalt as if lit from within.

Barnaby tugged at his leash, but I stood motionless.

Once in a while, in the midst of an ordinary day, an object or action will take on transcendent meaning. I once got out of a taxi a block from my destination to give it to a man who seemed unusually frantic in his attempts to flag down a cab. "Hey, you look like you need a ride," I said as I climbed out. He looked at me and said, "Bless you," with such intensity that sometimes I wonder if getting out of that cab was the most virtuous thing I've ever done.

And in the moment that I waited beside the traffic light, I glimpsed the *ordinary* take the form of the *sublime*. That orange cone was the most real thing I'd ever seen.

As I looked, it seemed as though the usual street furniture—the mailbox, the trash can, the parked cars—withdrew in reverence. The cone stood as if it had stood there forever, part of the street and the city. Its shape was at once ancient and modern. Somehow, like a haystack, a park bench, a scholar's rock, or sea glass, it looked both man-made and a product of the natural, living world.

And its *color*. I stood transfixed by the luminous orange.

As I gazed, I felt lifted up, raised from my nagging worries and self-doubts into the timeless realm of pure sensation. But I wasn't experiencing the echoing magnificence of a museum or the remote beauty of a mountaintop; somehow, the presence of the traffic cone made the street feel more inviting, more full of possibilities. The cone seemed to shine with the very joy of its existence.

Around the cone, every sight, every sound, seemed amplified. I felt the sharp icy breeze sweep the hair out of my face, I smelled the warm wool from my scarf mixed with the ozone-and-salt scent of the damp pavement, and I heard murmurs of conversation from a couple walking past me.

And the impressions that rose into my mind as I gazed at that cone were just as intense as the sensations of my body. In this moment, I felt a sudden affection toward the people around me, with a tenderness that expanded to encircle the world—all those *people*! With all their faces, songs, jokes, and luck. Nothing matters more to me than people.

I was wide-awake, with so much sensation pouring in that I felt electrified by it. Then, with a fresh gust of wind, rain began to fall, the light from the sky darkened, and the traffic cone faded back into an ordinary street object.

The moment passed—but it lives again now, and will again, and will forever, or at least for as long as I live.

Look, look, look! *Stretch out your hand.*

Acknowledgments

With every book I write, I think, "Well, this book is the high point. Never again will I find such an interesting subject." And then I do.

I have so many people to thank for their help and insights.

Thanks, first, to librarians, booksellers, readers, and podcast listeners; I so appreciate your enthusiasm and support.

In particular, I want to give a special thanks to the readers and listeners who have contacted me with questions, ideas, and suggested resources. I've learned so much from our conversations, and many of your observations made their way into this book. Special thanks to Finn Duggan, Reem Kassis, Chuck Reed, and Sarah Sze for talking to me about their particular sensory experiences.

So many people help me put my words out into the world.

Thanks to my outstanding agent, Christy Fletcher of Fletcher & Co., and to Melissa Chinchillo, Sarah Fuentes, and Yona Levin, and also Victoria Hobbs.

Thanks to my editor, Mary Reynics, for her superb guidance, and also to the terrific Crown team: Gillian Blake, Sarah Breivogel, Gina

Centrello, Julie Cepler, David Drake, Christina Foxley, Emily Hartley, Lindsey Kennedy, and Annsley Rosner. Thanks, too, to the Two Roads team.

And thanks as well to Crystal Ellefsen, Delia Lloyd, and especially Alice Truax.

Heartfelt thanks to the brilliant, imaginative team of Gretchen Rubin Media: Adam Caswell, Lauren Christensen, Annie Jolley, Emy Joyeux, Jason Konrad, Lindsay Logan, Anne Mercogliano, Joe Wadlington, and Hannah Wilson. Every day, it makes me happy to work with you.

Thanks to the terrific people who work with me on the *Happier with Gretchen Rubin* podcast: Chuck Reed and everyone at Cadence 13, and Ben Davis at WME.

Thanks to my writers' groups for all the good counsel and commiseration.

Many thanks to the institutions and supporters of the Metropolitan Museum, Central Park, and the New York Society Library. I never take these extraordinary places for granted.

Last of all, once again, thanks to my friends and family—Karen Craft, Jack Craft, Elizabeth Craft, Judy Rubin, and Bob Rubin, and for this book, especially Jamie, Eliza, and Eleanor—who have cheerfully offered themselves as guinea pigs in so many of my self-experiments.

Try This at Home

A Five-Senses Jump-Start

I hope that reading about my experiments and experiences will have you springing out of your seat to engage with your own senses.

To help you better understand your own relationship to your senses, I've created quizzes at gretchenrubin.com/quiz/.

Also, I've created this guide as a jump-start.

Generally, these exercises help to . . .

- explore a sense using an experiment or illusion
- share a sense-experience with others
- plan an adventure around a sense-experience
- reflect on memories sparked by a sensation
- boost the pleasures we get from a sense, or reduce any annoyances
- deepen a sense-experience through education
- create something inspired by a sense-experience
- indulge in a modest splurge to enjoy a sensation

- notice the ordinary
- identify a healthy treat

I'm always adding to my list, so please send me any suggestions.

Seeing

- Explore your sense of sight with some online experiments:
  —Look up "the dress" to see if it looks white and gold or black and blue to you.
  —Watch a video illustrating the McGurk effect.
  —Watch the Monkey Business Illusion video.
- Look for what's overlooked. Television advertisements, drugstore shelves, logos, book jackets, your office, the houses on your street . . . What do you notice when you really look closely?
- Choose a place for a daily visit. You might hike the same trail, take the same walk through your neighborhood, visit the same grocery store, or sit on the same bench overlooking a garden. Is there a place in your life that you've always wanted to explore more deeply? When we visit a place every day, we see it differently.
- Indulge in a splurge of color. Find an inexpensive, easy way to add a beautiful spot of color—wear a bright, fun color; paint the back of a cabinet; add a paperweight to your desk; buy a set of colored pencils; paint your nails.
- Collect a color. Find ways to mass a favorite color together. Create shelves of books that have that color on their spines, or consider nature as a source (pinecones, shells, feathers). Each year, my mother decorates a tree with nothing but Santa ornaments, all with the same red-white-and-black color scheme, and it looks spectacular.
- Offer a sensation invitation by inviting someone to join you for a sight-based adventure. A waterfall, a new neighborhood, a

historic site . . . Sightseeing is one of the most popular ways to share an experience with someone.

• Find new ways to see. To sharpen your sense of sight, choose an object and try to see it in many ways: Look at it in a mirror, squint at it, block part of it with your hand, look for shifts in scale, look at it from far away and close up.

• Immerse yourself in sight. Seek out an experience that over-whelms your sense of sight: a planetarium, an IMAX movie, Las Vegas.

• Make your smartphone screen less appealing by switching it to "grayscale." For a day or a week, set your phone to display in black, white, and gray to see how the lack of color affects your usage.

• Or make your smartphone screen more appealing by updating your home-screen image, organizing your apps, and cleaning out any apps you don't need.

• Collect postcards of sights you enjoy and add them to your surroundings: Place them in drawers where you'll come across them unexpectedly, mix them in with the papers in your inbox, put a few atop your car's sun visor so that you can pull one down when you're stuck in traffic.

• Eliminate an eyesore. Look around your home and office. Can you spot any areas that are cluttered, crowded, shabby, or dirty, or otherwise hurt your eyes? Figure out a plan to make improvements.

• Pay attention to eyes and gaze. Notice the power of eye con-tact and how much you can guess about other people's thoughts by tracking their gaze. Hold someone's eyes for thirty seconds to feel the intensity of gaze.

• Look for faces—on the fronts of cars, in the bark of trees, in the pattern on your slice of toast.

• Let your mind off the leash. Give yourself the opportunity to wander around without trying to direct your thoughts.

Hearing

- Explore your sense of hearing with some online experiments:
    —Listen to the "Virtual Barber Shop."
    —Listen to the Shepard tone.
    —Determine whether you hear "Laurel" or "Yanny."
- Consider your relationship to music—how you prefer to listen, to what kinds of songs and to what kinds of music. Are you a song lover or a music lover?
- Create an Audio Apothecary. Make a list of songs you love, for whatever state of mind you'd like to cultivate. Maybe you'd like a playlist that puts you in a happy, high-energy mood—or perhaps you'd like songs that invoke a calm, reflective spirit or a yearning, melancholy mood. Music can be a terrific way to give ourselves a treat.
- Attend a concert, try a sound bath. While it's wonderful to have so much recorded sound available to us, nothing replaces the experience of a live performance.
- Download a birdsong-identification app and identify the birds around you.
- Take the microphone; that is, look for ways to show consideration for people who have different experiences of the sensory world.
- Pay attention to your listening. Write your own Manifesto for Listening to remind yourself of your own listening challenges— and how you might listen better.
- Listen to music to create your own personal soundtrack as you move through your day. Notice how music can influence your mood.
- Improve the sounds associated with your smartphone. Choose a more pleasant alarm tone, assign a custom ring or text tone to people who are important to you, turn off unnecessary notifications.
- Notice a particular moment. Pause and really *listen*. What sounds do you hear? How do those sounds change your experi-

ence of a place and situation? What sounds are so familiar that they barely register?

• Turn down the noise. Just as you might clear clutter, find ways to clear clatter. Eliminate earsores and protect your ears: Turn off your phone notifications, invest in noise-canceling earbuds or headphones, turn off the TV if you're not watching it, and avoid noisy places.

• Go online to compare the different "colors" of noise. Which do you prefer? Might you benefit from using white, pink, green, or other background noise to sleep better, concentrate more deeply, or calm down?

• Turn up the silence. If possible, carve out some time for restorative silence, when you don't talk to anyone, don't watch movies or TV, and don't listen to music or podcasts. If you find the silence restful, look for ways to incorporate more silence into your life.

• Make voice recordings of the people you love.

• Get grounded in your body. If you're feeling anxious, upset, or angry, tune in to the experience of your five senses, right here, right now.

Smelling

• Explore your sense of smell with some home experiments:
  —Plug your nose and put a jelly bean in your mouth, then unplug your nose and note how the flavor changes.
  —Try a board game like Follow Your Nose or team up with others to try to identify mystery scents.
  —Notice how even a strong smell fades out of awareness after a few minutes.
  —Compare how each nostril registers a slightly different smell.

• Sharpen your sense of smell by increasing blood flow to your nose—run up and down stairs or do some jumping jacks.

• Go out of your way to have interesting smell experiences. Smell items such as smelling salts, scratch-and-sniffs, and unfamiliar fruits.

• As you experience a scent, try to describe the experience. Do you smell something floral, fruity, sweet, green, fresh, light, heavy, cool, warm, bright, delicate, animalic, powdery, herbal, medicinal, woody, sour, minty, rancid, dusty, urinous, buttery, smoky, vegetal, resinous?

• Add fragrance. Look for ways to add a beautiful scent to your environment: scented candles, sachets, fresh flowers, perfume, incense sticks. If, out of consideration for others, you don't wear perfume or cologne during the day, try wearing it at night.

• Eliminate odor. Find ways to fix something smelly: the fridge, the space under the kitchen sink, a trash bin, a dank basement, a mildewy shower curtain, a carpet subjected to lots of pet accidents.

• Pay attention to the smells of places you visit: the lobby of an office building, a pet store, a classroom. The familiar is easy to ignore.

• Identify and capture a strong scent memory.

• Pay attention to the smell of a person you love.

• To feel more present in a particular place and time, pause to notice all the smells you can detect.

Tasting

• Explore your sense of taste with some home experiments:
  —Use an orange to experience the difference between sour and bitter: The segments taste sour and the rind tastes bitter.
  —Try the miracle fruit that makes sour things taste sweet.
  —Try Szechuan buttons that create a buzzing, numb sensation.
  —Cook with spices you haven't used before.

• Write a Tastes Timeline of your life. What flavors do you most associate with different periods? You may want to reminisce with family or friends. What did you taste most often? What were your favorite (or least favorite) tastes? If you can, revisit a family recipe, restaurant, or ingredient that holds memories.

• Explore tastes from around the world by visiting an international market. Choose a few items to try.

• Pull out a bottle of ketchup and pay close attention as you put a few drops on your tongue. Notice its taste and also its color and shine, its smell, its texture. Now try ketchup with another food. How does it change the flavor you experience? Now try vanilla—breathe in its scent, taste a drop, notice how it enhances flavors when you add it.

• Deprive yourself of a common taste for a day, a week, a month, indefinitely. Deprivation can help remind us of the pleasure that we get from a taste by temporarily giving it up; deprivation may also show us that we're happier when we give up a taste altogether.

• Educate your tongue. Take a tasting class, in person or online, to learn about some taste that interests you, such as wine, beer, cheese, chocolate, or coffee. Better yet, take a class with someone else.

• Hold a taste party. Invite people to compare tastes of different brands or varieties of familiar items, such as fruits, vinegars, olives, teas, nut butters, pickles, milks, and energy bars; to identify mystery tastes; or to appreciate a common item or ingredient that's taken for granted.

• Explore a taste yourself. Identify something you often eat or drink, and compare different varieties to sharpen your perception.

• Share taste memories. Our sense of taste offers us a great way to connect with others—their childhoods, their cultures,

their memories. Invite someone you love to share their experiences around food and eating, and sample those tastes together.
• Invent a new variety of ice cream, sandwich, or other dish.
• Seek an experience that will give you some boredom. Boredom can stimulate our imaginations, because when we're bored, we reach inward to find stimulation.

Touching

• Explore your sense of touch with some home experiments:
  —Pull out some cornstarch to squeak it between your fingers. Then add water to create a non-Newtonian fluid that feels both liquid and solid.
  —Play with a touch-based toy: kinetic sand, Play-Doh, Silly Putty, modeling clay. Fold a paper airplane, fortune-teller, or origami figure.
  —Search for interesting textures and materials in your everyday life, with tinfoil, sandpaper, or plants such as a cactus or a lamb's ear plant.
• Use your sense of touch to engage with books that have a touch element, such as "touch and feel" books, pop-up books, and lift-the-flap books.
• Visit a store where you can touch the merchandise. Feel the plushy folds of bath towels, the smooth surface of glass mixing bowls, the cold weight of carpentry tools.
• As you move through your day, touch as many textures as possible and notice how your entire experience changes when you use your hands.
• Give a loving touch. Within appropriate bounds, of course, look for opportunities for affectionate hugs, fist bumps, squeezes, hand-holding, or quick touches. Find ways to connect with the people you love through a warm touch.
• Pet animals, and really notice the texture of their fur and bodies.

- Hold a calming prop, such as a mug, a pen, a clipboard, or a stone. Some touch items are specifically designed to help boost calm and focus, so consider trying a weighted blanket, therapy dough, a popping fidget toy, or a fidget spinner.
- Drench your sense of touch in a bath, shower, sensory deprivation tank, lake, or the ocean.
- Consider which textures please you or bother you: silky, velvety, plushy, rough, nubbly, scratchy, stiff, gritty, slick.
- Touch the intangible by identifying a lucky object to hold or a lucky ritual to perform.
- Use your hands to ignite your imagination. Translate some abstract concept into physical form, to help you grapple with it more effectively.
- With a "sensorium gift," give someone an experience by designing a gift based on the pleasures and comfort of the five senses.
- Buy the gift-shop version of some artwork you admire—mug, calendar, coaster—and notice how the experience of possessing it alters your view of the piece.
- On a visit to a museum, buy a few postcards of artwork on display, then visit them to compare the actual artwork to the postcard version. Notice how looking at the postcard changes your view of the real piece.

Five Senses

- For more delight: To notice and appreciate your five senses, keep a Five-Senses Journal where each day, you note the sense-highlights you experience. Delight others by playing a lighthearted prank or giving a gift that confounds the senses. If you're not yet twenty-five years old, expose yourself to as many new sensations as possible; if we haven't had a positive experience with something like a new food or new form of music by that age, we probably won't embrace it.

- For more love: To draw closer to someone you love, create a Five-Senses Portrait, to push yourself to notice small details of that person's physical presence. You might also use this exercise to help you remember and celebrate a person who has died, or to hang on to memories of a place, a season of the year, or a particular experience.

- For more energy and calm: Depending on what works for you, turn sensations up or down to refresh your mind.

- For more imagination: To give yourself some unstructured time to play, schedule time for recess. Visit a place that sells materials and tools for creative endeavors: a hardware store, department store, home-improvement store, gardening center, farmers market, cooking-supply store, art store, or craft store.

- For more memories: One day, *now* will be a long time ago, so to sharpen your experience of the present, and to create memories for the future, create an Album of Now by making a photo album of your ordinary life. Search real estate websites to look for photographs of places from your past.

- For more self-knowledge: Visit a place that fills you with awe and open your senses to experience it.

Further Resources

I hope that *Life in Five Senses* has given you many ideas about how to engage with your own five senses.

For more, visit my website, gretchenrubin.com, where I post regularly about my adventures in happiness, the five senses, good habits, and human nature. There, I write about the many five-senses experiments that I tried but didn't include in this book.

For many additional resources, such as a discussion guide, visit my site, gretchenrubin.com.

Learn more about your relationship to your senses by taking a five-senses quiz: gretchenrubin.com/quiz/.

If you'd like to listen to my Audio Apothecary for yourself, you can find it on Spotify.

Sign up for my popular, free weekly newsletter "5 Things Making Me Happy" at gretchenrubin.com/newsletters/, or sign up for the free "Moment of Happiness" for a daily quotation at gretchenrubin .com/quotations/. (More than one million people get my newsletters.)

Listen to the weekly *Happier with Gretchen Rubin* podcast, where my sister Elizabeth and I reveal fresh insights from cutting-edge science, ancient wisdom, pop culture, and our own experiences about how to be happier.

Subscribe to the Happier app, an award-winning habit-tracking app that provides personalized strategies to help you become happier, healthier, more productive, and more creative. To learn more and sign up, go to thehappierapp.com.

Join the conversation by following @gretchenrubin on . . .

Instagram
Facebook
Twitter
YouTube
LinkedIn
Goodreads
TikTok

Email me about your own experiences, insights, and questions through my site, gretchenrubin.com.

I look forward to hearing from you about this endlessly fascinating subject: the practice of everyday life.

—Gretchen Rubin

Notes

While I've changed a few names for privacy, edited some comments for clarity, and reordered some incidents—especially given the massive disruption caused by Covid-19—all accounts come from real people and actual events.

Coming to My Senses

13   **"I listened and there was a buzz":** Andy Warhol, *The Philosophy of Andy Warhol (From A to B and Back Again)* (New York: Harvest, 1975), 219.

14   **"Every man's spice-box":** Zora Neale Hurston, *Dust Tracks on a Road: An Autobiography* (New York: J. B. Lippincott, 1942), 69.

14   **In his memoir:** Gerald Shea, *Songs Without Words: Discovering My Deafness Halfway Through Life* (New York: Da Capo Press, 2013).

15   **"My own eyes were needed":** Simone de Beauvoir, *Memoirs of a Dutiful Daughter* (New York: Harper Perennial, 1958), 125.

18   **Research shows that happier people:** Sonja Lyubomirsky, Laura King, and Ed Diener, "The Benefits of Frequent Positive Affect: Does Happiness Lead to Success?," *Psychological Bulletin* 131, no. 6 (2005): 803–55.

19   **"Live as long as you may":** Robert Southey, quoted in T. W.
        Brown, *Early Called: A Memoir of William Deans* (London: James
        Nisbet, 1869), 174.

                                    Seeing

25   **"I'm a capable blind man":** Stephen Kuusisto, *Eavesdropping: A
        Memoir of Blindness and Listening* (New York: W. W. Norton,
        2006), 63; see also Stephen Kuusisto, *Have Dog, Will Travel: A
        Poet's Journey* (New York: Simon & Schuster, 2018).

31   **"The goal of all art":** Paul Cézanne, quoted in Ambroise Vollard,
        Cézanne (New York: Dover Publications, 1984).

31   **when three-year-olds are asked:** Margaret S. Livingstone, *Vision
        and Art: The Biology of Seeing,* rev. and expanded ed., foreword by
        David Hubel (New York: Abrams, 2014), 206.

33   **Katy Perry, Tori Spelling:** Reed Tucker, "Stare Wars," *New York
        Post,* May 29, 2011.

34   **after about four seconds:** Nicola Binetti, Charlotte Harrison,
        Antoine Coutrot, et al., "Pupil Dilation as an Index of Preferred
        Mutual Gaze Duration," *Royal Society Open Science* 3, no. 7 (July
        2016).

35   **"Anything one does every day":** Gertrude Stein, *Paris France*
        (New York: W. W. Norton, 1940), 21.

36   **The brain—like the rest of the body:** John Medina, *Brain
        Rules: 12 Principles for Surviving and Thriving at Work, Home, and
        School* (Seattle: Pear Press, 2014), 13–22; Marily Oppezzo and
        Daniel L. Schwartz, "Give Your Ideas Some Legs: The Positive
        Effect of Walking on Creative Thinking," *Journal of Experimental
        Psychology* 40, no. 4 (2014): 1142–52.

38   **Research shows that the design of spaces:** Annie Murphy
        Paul, *The Extended Mind: The Power of Thinking Outside the Brain*
        (New York: Mariner Books, 2021), 128–38.

40   **"Color slips through the fingers":** Derek Jarman, *Chroma: A
        Book of Color* (New York: Overlook Press, 1995), 23.

40   **painting a jail cell:** Oliver Genschow, Thomas Noll, Michaela
        Wanke, and Robert Gersbach, "Does Baker-Miller Pink Reduce
        Aggression in Prison Detention Cells? A Critical Empirical Exami-
        nation," *Psychology, Crime & Law* 21, no. 5 (2014): 482–89;
        Charles Spence, *Sensehacking: How to Use the Power of Your Senses
        for Happier, Healthier Living* (New York: Viking, 2021), 32.

Hearing

67   **When the Beatles exploded in popularity:** David Howes and
      Constance Classen, *Ways of Sensing: Understanding the Senses in
      Society* (New York: Routledge, 2014), 2.

67   **If we're older:** Paul Bloom, *How Pleasure Works: The New Science
      of Why We Like What We Like* (New York: W. W. Norton, 2010),
      128.

79   **Renowned French actress Emmanuelle Laborit:** Emmanuelle
      Laborit, *The Cry of the Gull,* trans. Constantina Mitchell and Paul
      Raymond Côté (Washington, D.C.: Gallaudet University Press,
      1994), 33.

81   **as much as 20 percent:** Lawrence D. Rosenblum, *See What I'm
      Saying: The Extraordinary Powers of Our Five Senses* (New York:
      W. W. Norton, 2011), 248–49.

81   **For adults, research has found:** Kate Murphy, *You're Not Listen-
      ing: What You're Missing and Why It Matters* (New York: Celadon
      Books / Macmillan, 2019), 148.

81   **this pattern is fairly inevitable:** Jaimie Arona Krems and Jason
      Wilkes, "Why Are Conversations Limited to About Four People? A
      Theoretical Exploration of the Conversation Size Constraint," *Evo-
      lution and Human Behavior* 40, no. 2 (March 2019): 140–47.

83   **the mere presence of a phone:** Murphy, *You're Not Listening,*
      176.

87   **Noisy hospitals make it harder:** Katie Jue and Dan Nathan-
      Roberts, "How Noise Affects Patients in Hospitals," *Proceedings of
      the Human Factors and Ergonomics Society Annual Meeting* 63,
      no. 1 (2019): 1510–14.

87   **no matter what our age:** Seth S. Horowitz, *The Universal Sense:
      How Hearing Shapes the Mind* (New York: Bloomsbury, 2012),
      118.

89   **research also suggests that loud noise:** Barb Stuckey, *Taste
      What You're Missing: Surprising Stories and Science About Why Food
      Tastes Good* (New York: Atria, 2013), 118–19.

89   **some 7-Eleven and Rite Aid stores:** Benjamin Oreskes, "To
      Chase Away Homeless People, 7-Eleven Stores in L.A. Use Classi-
      cal Music," *Los Angeles Times,* September 6, 2019; Kim Baldonado,
      "SoCal Rite Aids Use Barry Manilow Music to Discourage Loiter-
      ing," *NBC Los Angeles,* June 30, 2018.

91 **the average person:** Matthias R. Mehl, Simine Vazire, Nairán Ramírez-Esparza, et al., "Are Women Really More Talkative Than Men?," *Science* 317 (July 2007): 82.

Smelling

100 **When the Department of Defense:** Randall Munroe, "What's the World's Worst Smell?," *New York Times,* February 26, 2020.

101 **As "smell scientist":** Avery N. Gilbert, *What the Nose Knows: The Science of Scent in Everyday Life* (New York: Synesthetics Inc., 2014), 86.

113 **He'd wear a perfume:** Andy Warhol, *The Philosophy of Andy Warhol (From A to B and Back Again)* (New York: Harvest, 1975), 151.

115 **"I love a broad margin":** Henry David Thoreau, *Walden and Other Writings* (New York: Modern Library, 1992), 105.

Tasting

125 **Cooking icon Julia Child:** Joan Reardon, *As Always, Julia: The Letters of Julia Child and Avis DeVoto* (New York: Mariner Books, 2011), 31.

125 **food essayist Jean Anthelme:** Jean Anthelme Brillat-Savarin, *The Physiology of Taste,* translated by M.F.K. Fisher (New York: Vintage Books, 2011), 15.

129 **we associate the color blue:** Charles Spence and Betina Piqueras-Fiszman, *The Perfect Meal: The Multisensory Science of Food and Dining* (Oxford: John Wiley & Sons, 2014), 116.

129 **In one study:** Bob Holmes, *Flavor: The Science of Our Most Neglected Sense* (New York: W. W. Norton, 2017), 111.

129 **people were asked to rate:** Mike Pomranz, "Corks Make Wine Taste Better, According to the Results of This Experiment," *Food & Wine,* September 27, 2017.

135 **In what's called the "reminiscence bump":** Jennifer Senior, "Why You Never Truly Leave High School," *New York,* January 18, 2013.

136 **As Proust observes:** Marcel Proust, *Swann's Way,* trans. C. K. Scott Moncrieff (New York: Vintage Books, 1982), 27.

137 **Heinz ketchup is the rare food:** Malcolm Gladwell, "The Ketchup Conundrum," *The New Yorker,* August 29, 2004.

139 **In East Asia, where vanilla:** Amy Fleming, "The Geography of Taste: How Our Food Preferences Are Formed," *The Guardian,* September 3, 2013.

139 **Most flavors taste good:** Stuckey, *Taste,* 206.

141   **As Brillat-Savarin remarked:** Jean Anthelme Brillat-Savarin, *The Physiology of Taste,* translated by M.F.K. Fisher (New York: Vintage Books, 2011), 15.

148   **It came on the scene:** Raffi Khatchadourian, "The Taste Makers: The Secret World of the Flavor Factory," *The New Yorker,* November 15, 2009.

156   **"There are children":** Gaston Bachelard, *The Poetics of Space* (New York: Penguin Books, 1958), 17.

157   **the more we create:** Scott Barry Kaufman, "Why Creativity Is a Numbers Game," *Scientific American,* December 29, 2015.

161   **"Life is barren enough":** Samuel Johnson, quoted in Hesther Lynch Piozzi, *Anecdotes of Samuel Johnson* (Cambridge: Cambridge University Press, 1932), 191.

Touching

168   **"Cease to use your hands":** George Orwell, *The Road to Wigan Pier* (New York: Mariner Books, 1972), 197.

168   **"If we pick up a brush":** Yoshida Kenkō, *Essays in Idleness,* trans. Donald Keene (New York: Columbia University Press, 1967), 139.

169   **Cunning marketers tempt us to touch:** Joann Peck and Suzanne Shu, "The Effect of Mere Touch on Perceived Ownership," *Journal of Consumer Research* 36, no. 3 (2009): 434–47.

172   **a ten-minute encounter:** Ben Carey, Colleen Anne Dell, James Stempien, et al., "Outcomes of a Controlled Trial with Visiting Therapy Dog Teams on Pain in Adults in an Emergency Department," *PLoS ONE* 17, no. 3 (February 2021): e0262599.

179   **"Touch has its ecstasies":** Helen Keller, *The World I Live In* (New York: Floating Press, 2013), 16.

182   **The theory of "embodied cognition":** Paul, *The Extended Mind,* 53–54, 156–59.

183   **Some came from great artists:** James Baldwin, quoted in Fred R. Standley and Darnell D. Pratt, eds., *Conversations with James Baldwin* (Jackson: University Press of Mississippi, 1989), 245; Twyla Tharp, *The Creative Habit: Learn It and Use It for Life* (New York: Simon & Schuster, 2003), 78–92.

Onward

196   **"There is no greater sign":** Samuel Butler, *The Note-Books of Samuel Butler* (London: A. C. Fifield, 1921), 259.

196   ***"Look at me!":*** Dr. Seuss, *The Cat in the Hat* (New York: Random House, 1957), 18.

197   **taking photos actually helps:** Kristin Diehl, Gal Zauberman, and
        Alixandra Barasch, "How Taking Photos Increases Enjoyment of
        Experiences," *Journal of Personality and Social Psychology* 11, no. 2
        (2016): 119–40.

204   **"If someone asked me":** May Sarton, *Plant Dreaming Deep* (New
        York: W. W. Norton, 1968), 122.

205   **"My mind works in idleness":** Virginia Woolf, *A Writer's Diary*
        (New York: Mariner Books, 2003), 151.

206   **"The creative mind plays":** Carl Jung, *The Collected Works of
        C. G. Jung,* vol. 6, *Psychological Types* (Princeton, N.J.: Princeton
        University Press, 1971), 123.

207   **In 2012, to make mandatory cigarette packaging:** Carey
        Dunne, "In Defense of the World's Ugliest Color, 'Opaque
        Couché,'" *Hyperallergic,* June 16, 2016.

212   **"I find it harder":** Oscar Wilde, quoted in Richard Ellmann,
        Oscar Wilde (New York: Vintage Books, 1987), 45.

Suggestions for Further Reading

Many extraordinary books have been written about the five senses. This list doesn't attempt to cover all the most important works but instead highlights some of my personal favorites.

General

Ackerman, Diane. *A Natural History of the Senses*. New York: Vintage Books, 1991.

Brown, Darren. *Tricks of the Mind*. London: Transworld, 2006.

Bryson, Bill. *The Body: A Guide for Occupants*. New York: Anchor, 2021.

Dehaene, Stanislas. *How We Learn: Why Brains Learn Better Than Any Machine . . . For Now*. New York: Penguin, 2021.

———. *The Number Sense: How the Mind Creates Mathematics*. New York: Oxford University Press, 1997.

———. *Reading in the Brain: The New Science of How We Read*. New York: Penguin, 2009.

Dutton, Denis. *The Art Instinct: Beauty, Pleasure, and Human Evolution*. New York: Bloomsbury Press, 2010.

Eagleman, David. *Incognito: The Secret Lives of the Brain*. New York: Vintage Books, 2012.

———. *Livewired: The Inside Story of the Ever-Changing Brain*. New York: Pantheon, 2020.

Grandin, Temple. *Visual Thinking: The Hidden Gifts of People Who Think in Pictures, Patterns, and Abstractions*. New York: Riverhead, 2022.

Higgins, Jackie. *Sentient: How Animals Illuminate the Wonder of Our Human Senses*. New York: Atria, 2022.

Howes, David, and Constance Classen. *Ways of Sensing: Understanding the Senses in Society*. New York: Routledge, 2014.

Hurston, Zora Neale. *Dust Tracks on a Road: An Autobiography*. New York: J. B. Lippincott, 1942.

Konigsburg, E. L. *From the Mixed-Up Files of Mrs. Basil E. Frankweiler*. New York: Atheneum, 1998.

Ladau, Emily. *Demystifying Disability: What to Know, What to Say, and How to Be an Ally*. New York: Ten Speed Press, 2021.

Lee, Ingrid Fetell. *Joyful: The Surprising Power of Ordinary Things to Create Extraordinary Happiness*. New York: Little, Brown Spark, 2018.

Lieberman, Daniel. *The Story of the Human Body: Evolution, Health, and Disease*. New York: Vintage, 2014.

Lieberman, Matthew. *Social: Why Our Brains Are Wired to Connect*. New York: Crown, 2014.

Paul, Annie Murphy. *The Extended Mind: The Power of Thinking Outside the Brain*. New York: Mariner Books, 2021.

Spence, Charles. *Sensehacking: How to Use the Power of Your Senses for Happier, Healthier Living*. New York: Viking Books, 2021.

Temkin, Ann. *Color Chart: Reinventing Color: 1950 to Today*. New York: Museum of Modern Art, 2008.

Tversky, Barbara. *Mind in Motion: How Action Shapes Thought*. New York: Basic Books, 2019.

Warhol, Andy. *The Philosophy of Andy Warhol (From A to B and Back Again)*. New York: Harvest, 1975.

Wong, Alice, ed. *Disability Visibility: First-Person Stories from the Twentieth Century*. New York: Vintage Books, 2020.

Yong, Ed. *An Immense World: How Animal Senses Reveal the Hidden Realms Around Us*. New York: Random House, 2022.

Young, Emma. *Super Senses: The Science of Your 32 Senses and How to Use Them*. New York: John Murray, 2021.

Seeing

Barry, Susan R. *Fixing My Gaze: A Scientist's Journey into Seeing in Three Dimensions*. New York: Basic Books, 2010.

Bruni, Frank. *The Beauty of Dusk: On Vision Lost and Found*. New York: Avid Reader Press / Simon & Schuster, 2022.

Grunwald, Henry. *Twilight: Losing Sight, Gaining Insight*. New York: Vintage Books, 2012.

Knighton, Ryan. *Cockeyed: A Memoir of Blindness*. New York: PublicAffairs, 2007.

Kuusisto, Stephen. *Eavesdropping: A Memoir of Blindness and Listening*. New York: W. W. Norton, 2006.

———. *Have Dog, Will Travel: A Poet's Journey*. New York: Simon & Schuster, 2018.

———. *Planet of the Blind: A Memoir*. New York: Delta, 1998.

Lidsky, Isaac. *Eyes Wide Open: Overcoming Obstacles and Recognizing Opportunities in a World That Can't See Clearly*. New York: TarcherPerigee, 2017.

Livingstone, Margaret S. *Vision and Art: The Biology of Seeing*. Revised and expanded edition. Foreword by David Hubel. New York: Abrams, 2014.

Mehta, Ved. *Dark Harbor: Building House and Home on an Enchanted Island*. New York: Nation Books, 2003.

Pastoureau, Michel. *Black: The History of a Color*. Princeton, N.J.: Princeton University Press, 2008.

———. *Blue: The History of a Color*. Princeton, N.J.: Princeton University Press, 2018.

———. *The Devil's Cloth: A History of Stripes*. New York: Washington Square Press, 2003.

———. *Green: The History of a Color*. Princeton, N.J.: Princeton University Press, 2014.

———. *Red: The History of a Color*. Princeton, N.J.: Princeton University Press, 2017.

———. *Yellow: The History of a Color*. Princeton, N.J.: Princeton University Press, 2019.

St. Clair, Kassia. *The Secret Lives of Color*. New York: Penguin, 2017.

Hearing

Bouton, Katherine. *Shouting Won't Help: Why I—and 50 Million Other Americans—Can't Hear You*. New York: Picador, 2014.

Colapinto, John. *This Is the Voice*. New York: Simon & Schuster, 2022.

Cox, Trevor. *Now You're Talking: Human Conversation from the Neanderthals to Artificial Intelligence*. New York: Counterpoint, 2018.

DiMarco, Nyle. *Deaf Utopia: A Memoir—and a Love Letter to a Way of Life*. New York: William Morrow, 2022.

Drolsbaugh, Mark. *Deaf Again: Born into Deaf Culture, Thrown into the Hearing World, Rediscovering the Joys of Deafness*. Springhouse, Pa.: Handwave, 2019.

Dunbar, Robin. *Grooming, Gossip, and the Evolution of Language*. New York: Harvard University Press, 1997.

Karpf, Anne. *The Human Voice: How This Extraordinary Instrument Reveals Essential Clues About Who We Are*. New York: Bloomsbury, 2006.

Keizer, Garrett. *The Unwanted Sound of Everything We Want: A Book About Noise.* New York: PublicAffairs, 2010.

Laborit, Emmanuelle. *The Cry of the Gull.* Translated by Constantina Mitchell and Paul Raymond Côté. Washington, D.C.: Gallaudet University Press, 1994.

Levitin, Daniel. *This Is Your Brain on Music: The Science of a Human Obsession.* New York: Plume / Penguin, 2007.

Maitland, Sara. *A Book of Silence.* New York: Counterpoint, 2010.

Murphy, Kate. *You're Not Listening: What You're Missing and Why It Matters.* New York: Celadon Books / Macmillan, 2021.

Owen, David. *Volume Control: Hearing in a Deafening World.* New York: Riverhead, 2019.

Prochnik, George. *In Pursuit of Silence: Listening for Meaning in a World of Noise.* New York: Anchor Books, 2011.

Shea, Gerald. *Songs Without Words: Discovering My Deafness Halfway Through Life.* New York: Da Capo Press, 2013.

Thomas, Sue. *Silent Night.* New York: Tyndale House, 1990.

Smelling

Barwich, A. S. *Smellosophy: What the Nose Tells the Mind.* Cambridge, Mass.: Harvard University Press, 2020.

Blodgett, Bonnie. *Remembering Smell: A Memoir of Losing—and Discovering—the Primal Sense.* New York: Houghton Mifflin Harcourt, 2010.

Burr, Chandler. *The Perfect Scent: A Year Inside the Perfume Industry in Paris and New York.* New York: Picador, 2009.

Gilbert, Avery. *What the Nose Knows: The Science of Scent in Everyday Life.* New York: Synesthetics Inc., 2014.

Glaser, Gabrielle. *The Nose: A Profile of Sex, Beauty, and Survival.* New York: Atria, 2002.

Stewart, Jude. *Revelations in Air: A Guidebook to Smell.* New York: Penguin, 2021.

Tasting

Brillat-Savarin, Jean Anthelme. *The Physiology of Taste: Or Meditations on Transcendental Gastronomy*. New York: Vintage Books, 2011.

Fisher, M.F.K. *The Art of Eating*. New York: Harvest, 2004.

Herz, Rachel. *Why You Eat What You Eat: The Science Behind Our Relationship with Food*. New York: W. W. Norton, 2019.

Holmes, Bob. *Flavor: The Science of Our Most Neglected Sense*. New York: W. W. Norton, 2017.

McQuaid, John. *Tasty: The Art and Science of What We Eat*. New York: Scribner, 2016.

Miller, William. *The Anatomy of Disgust*. Cambridge, Mass.: Harvard University Press, 1998.

Pollan, Michael. *The Botany of Desire: A Plant's-Eye View of the World*. New York: Random House, 2002.

———. *How to Change Your Mind: What the New Science of Psychedelics Teaches Us About Consciousness, Dying, Addiction, Depression, and Transcendence*. New York: Penguin, 2019.

Roach, Mary. *Gulp: Adventures on the Alimentary Canal*. New York: W. W. Norton, 2013.

Segnit, Niki. *The Flavor Thesaurus: A Compendium of Pairings, Recipes and Ideas for the Creative Cook*. New York: Bloomsbury, 2012.

Shepherd, Gordon. *Neurogastronomy: How the Brain Creates Flavor and Why It Matters*. New York: Columbia University Press, 2013.

Spence, Charles, and Betina Piqueras-Fiszman. *The Perfect Meal: The Multisensory Science of Food and Dining*. Oxford: John Wiley & Sons, 2014.

Stuckey, Barb. *Taste What You're Missing: Surprising Stories and Science About Why Food Tastes Good*. New York: Atria, 2013.

Wilson, Bee. *First Bite: How We Learn to Eat*. New York: Basic Books, 2015.

Touching

Field, Tiffany. *Touch*. 2nd edition. Cambridge, Mass.: MIT Press, 2014.

Graziano, Michael. *The Spaces Between Us: A Story of Neuroscience, Evolution, and Human Nature*. New York: Oxford University Press, 2018.

Jablonski, Nina. *Skin: A Natural History*. Berkeley: University of California Press, 2006.

Linden, David. *Touch: The Science of Hand, Heart, and Mind*. New York: Penguin, 2016.

Subramanian, Sushma. *How to Feel: The Science and Meaning of Touch*. New York: Columbia University Press, 2021.

Trumble, Angus. *The Finger: A Handbook*. New York: Farrar, Straus and Giroux, 2010.

Wilson, Frank. *The Hand: How Its Use Shapes the Brain, Language, and Human Culture*. New York: Vintage Books, 1999.

List of Works from the Metropolitan Museum of Art

List of objects mentioned from the Metropolitan Museum of Art, New York.

Seeing

Lippi, Fra Filippo. *Portrait of a Woman with a Man at a Casement.* Ca. 1440. Tempera on wood. The Metropolitan Museum of Art, New York.

Bowl with Human Feet. Ca. 3700–3450 B.C. Pottery. The Metropolitan Museum of Art, New York.

Attributed to the Danaë Painter. *Terracotta Bell-Krater (bowl for mixing wine and water).* Ca. 460 B.C. Terracotta; red-figure. The Metropolitan Museum of Art, New York.

Panel with the Nativity. Ca. 1440. Pot metal, white glass, vitreous paint, silver stain. The Metropolitan Museum of Art, New York.

Hearing

Ngoma (drum). Vili or Yombe people. Nineteenth century. Wood, fiber, glass. The Metropolitan Museum of Art, New York.

Smelling

Mesu Smelling a Lotus. Ca. 1525-1504 B.C. Limestone. The Metropolitan Museum of Art, New York.

Pair of Eyes. Fifth century B.C. or later. Bronze, marble, frit, quartz, obsidian. The Metropolitan Museum of Art, New York.

Fragment of a Queen's Face. Ca. 1390–1336 B.C. Yellow jasper. The Metropolitan Museum of Art, New York.

Tasting

Johnson, Joshua. *Emma Van Name*. Ca. 1805. Oil on canvas. The Metropolitan Museum of Art, New York.

Touching

Durga as Slayer of the Buffalo Demon Mahishasura. Fourteenth-fifteenth century. Gilt copper alloy, inlaid with semiprecious stones. The Metropolitan Museum of Art, New York.

Patanazzi family workshop. *Inkstand with Apollo and the Muses*. 1584. Maiolica. The Metropolitan Museum of Art, New York.

Queen Mother Pendant Mask: Iyoba. Sixteenth century. Ivory, iron, copper(?). The Metropolitan Museum of Art, New York.

Bruegel the Elder, Pieter. *The Harvesters*. 1565. Oil on wood. The Metropolitan Museum of Art, New York.

Van Gogh, Vincent. *Self-Portrait with a Straw Hat*. 1887. Oil on canvas. The Metropolitan Museum of Art, New York.

Onward

God Horus Protecting King Nectanebo II. 360–343 B.C. Meta-Greywacke. The Metropolitan Museum of Art, New York.

About the Author

GRETCHEN RUBIN is one of today's most influential and thought-provoking observers of happiness and human nature. As a writer, she's known for her ability to distill and convey complex ideas—from science to literature to stories from her own life—with levity and clarity.

Rubin has cultivated a vast, passionate audience that actively engages with her and her work across many channels. With millions of copies of her *New York Times* bestselling books sold, more than 220 million downloads of her *Happier with Gretchen Rubin* podcast, the award-winning Happier app, imaginative products and tools, and an enthusiastic following on her newsletters and social media, she finds her audience wherever they want to be.

Rubin has been interviewed by Oprah Winfrey, eaten dinner with Nobel Prize winner Daniel Kahneman, walked arm in arm with the Dalai Lama, had her work reported on in a medical journal, been written up in *The New Yorker,* and been an answer on *Jeopardy!*

After starting her career in law, Rubin realized that she wanted to be a writer while she was clerking for Supreme Court justice Sandra Day O'Connor. Raised in Kansas City, she lives in New York City with her family.

gretchenrubin.com
facebook.com/GretchenRubin
Twitter: @gretchenrubin
Instagram: @gretchenrubin
TikTok: @gretchenrubin

My Five-Senses Self-Portrait
Gretchen Rubin

Seeing

1. The toothy cow grinning down from the stained-glass window in the Met
2. Jamie asleep under a heap of covers in early morning light
3. A wall of library shelves crowded with books
4. Clouds reflected in the water of the lake in Central Park
5. An orange traffic cone

Hearing

1. Eliza and Eleanor laughing at each other's jokes
2. Barnaby's deep sigh after he curls up on his favorite blanket
3. The faint clacking of fingers on a keyboard
4. Elizabeth saying, "Okay, Gretch, it's time for . . ." during a *Happier* recording
5. The roar of the #6 subway train as it pulls into the station

Smelling

1. Sharpie pens
2. Nighttime perfume
3. Black coffee
4. The Met's hand sanitizer
5. Crushed lavender

Tasting

1. Winstead's triple burger (plain, no bun)
2. Diet Coke
3. Eggs in many forms

4. Almonds
5. Sugar-free cinnamon mints

Touching

1. Plush terrycloth robe
2. A "family love sandwich" hug with Jamie, Eliza, and Eleanor
3. The almost imperceptible weight of contact lenses
4. Light wool fingertip-less gloves
5. A heavy mug warmed by a hot drink

About the Type

This book was set in Fairfield, the first typeface from the hand of the distinguished American artist and engraver Rudolph Ruzicka (1883–1978). Ruzicka was born in Bohemia (in the present-day Czech Republic) and came to America in 1894. He set up his own shop, devoted to wood engraving and printing, in New York in 1913 after a varied career working as a wood engraver, in photoengraving and banknote printing plants, and as an art director and freelance artist. He designed and illustrated many books and was the creator of a considerable list of individual prints—wood engravings, line engravings on copper, and aquatints.

"Look at the birds," he says. "Nothing can hold them. Not the Wall, nor the Gate, nor the sounding of the horn. It does good to watch the birds."
—Haruki Murakami,
*Hard-Boiled Wonderland
and the End of the World*

If you wish to make an apple pie from scratch, you must first invent the universe.
—Carl Sagan,
Cosmos: A Personal Voyage

There is no such thing as an empty space or an empty time. There is always something to see, something to hear.
—John Cage, *Silence*

It is the bell that moves, but you who ring. It is the sun that shines, but you who see.
—Joseph Joubert,
The Notebooks of Joseph Joubert

In the Hall of Gems at the Museum of Natural History in New York, I once stood in front of a huge piece of sulfur so yellow I began to cry.
—Diane Ackerman,
*A Natural History
of the Senses*

Here was peace. She pulled in her horizon like a great fish-net. Pulled it from around the waist of the world and draped it over her shoulder. So much of life in its meshes! She called in her soul to come and see.
—Zora Neale Hurston,
Their Eyes Were Watching God

Sugar cares only about itself, salt brings out the best in others.
—Karl Ove Knausgaard, *Summer*

There is no creature whose inward being is so strong that it is not greatly determined by what lies outside it.
—George Eliot, *Middlemarch*